ITBS® PREPARATION AND PRACTICE WORKBOOK

&

Ten Days to the ITBS®

Teacher's Annotated Edition

GRADE 6

Glencoe
McGraw-Hill

New York, New York   Columbus, Ohio   Woodland Hills, California   Peoria, Illinois

Iowa Tests of Basic Skills® is a trademark of Riverside Publishing Company. This book has been neither authorized nor endorsed by Riverside Publishing Company.

Grateful acknowledgment is given authors and publishers for permission to reprint the following copyrighted material. Every effort has been made to determine copyright owners. In case of any omissions, the Publisher will be pleased to make suitable acknowledgments in future editions.

Excerpt from "Red, White and Blue" by Yvette P. Fernandez, from *Icarus*, Fall 1993. Reprinted by permission.

Excerpt from *Accidents May Happen* by Charlotte Foltz Jones. Copyright © 1996 by Charlotte Foltz Jones. Reprinted by permission of Delacorte Press, a division of Random House, Inc.

"Trees: The Seeds" by Myra Cohn Livingston, from *Animal, Vegetable, Mineral*. Copyright © 1994 by Myra Cohn Livingston. Reprinted by permission of HarperCollins Publishers.

Excerpt from "A Model Family" by Ron Tanner. Reprinted by permission of the author.

Glencoe/McGraw-Hill

A Division of The McGraw-Hill Companies

Send all inquiries to:
Glencoe/McGraw-Hill
8787 Orion Place
Columbus, OH 43240

ISBN 0-07-821330-4

Printed in the United States of America

7 8 9 009 08 07

Table of Contents

Introduction

Annotated Preparation and Practice

Annotated Practice Test

Ten Days to the ITBS®

How This Book Is Organized

The ITBS® (which stands for *Iowa Tests of Basic Skills*) is a series of tests designed to assess student performance in Reading, Vocabulary, Math, Social Studies, and Science, among other subjects. This book concentrates on seven sections of the ITBS®: Vocabulary, Reading Comprehension, Spelling, Capitalization, Punctuation, Usage and Expression, and Reference Materials. These sections test students' ability to understand and process written information and to recognize the standards of written English. The bulk of this book—the *Ten Days to the ITBS®* section—focuses only on the Vocabulary and Reading Comprehension portions of the test. However, the *Preparation and Practice* Exercises will give students exposure to *all* the language arts sections included in the ITBS®.

The Student Edition of *Ten Days to the ITBS®* has three main sections: *Preparation and Practice* Exercises, the *Ten Days to the ITBS®* Practice Test, and *Ten Days to the ITBS®* Technique Lessons. The Teacher Edition of *Ten Days to the ITBS®* is organized to be used alongside the Student Edition. It includes the following sections:

1) **Teacher Introduction and Support Material**
   The introductory material includes a day-by-day syllabus, information on how to use this book, and other supporting material.

2) **Diagnostic Charts for Practice Test**
   The Student Diagnostic Chart breaks down answers by question type, allowing students to pinpoint their strengths and weaknesses. The Class Diagnostic Chart allows you to compile your students' results so that you can determine the areas in which your class as a whole might need more practice. Both charts cover only the Reading Comprehension section.

3) **Answer Bubble Sheet**
   The bubble sheet should be photocopied and passed out to students for use while taking the Practice Test. This will allow them to practice filling in their responses as they will on the actual ITBS®. Bubble sheets can also be used with the Exercises.

4) **Annotated *Preparation and Practice* Pages**
   The annotations provide correct answers and supplemental information to help you review these exercises with your students.

5) **Annotated Practice Test**
   The annotations provide correct answers and supplemental information to help you review this test with your students.

6) ***Ten Days to the ITBS®* Technique Lessons**
   These are reduced student pages with teacher wrap that includes analysis of question and answer types, instructional advice, explanation of technique processes, and helpful hints.

How to Use This Book

Preparation and Practice Exercises

For tests such as the ITBS®, it is best to begin preparing students early with short lessons. To this end, we have prepared a series of *Preparation and Practice* Exercises that should be given to your students at the completion of each unit in your textbook. These pages cover the Vocabulary, Reading Comprehension, Spelling, Capitalization, Punctuation, Usage and Expression, and Reference Materials sections of the ITBS®. Whenever possible, review these practice pages in detail with your students. Teacher annotations are included in this volume to aid you in this review process.

The *Ten Days to the ITBS®* Practice Test

As you near the test date, begin preparing students for the actual administration of the test by discussing the test format and timing. Before beginning the Technique Lessons, administer the *Ten Days to the ITBS®* Practice Test. Photocopy the bubble sheet (page 11) for your students' use, and administer the test under actual test conditions, giving students 55 minutes to complete it. We recommend that you administer the Practice Test approximately two to three weeks before the actual ITBS® test date.

The *Ten Days to the ITBS®* Technique Lessons

After the Practice Test has been administered and scored, you will be ready to teach the *Ten Days to the ITBS®* Technique Lessons. Before you start, ask students to fill out the Student Diagnostic Chart on pages 8–9. This chart divides up the Reading Comprehension questions into different types. Compiling your students' results on your Class Diagnostic Chart should give you a good idea of what areas need to be stressed.

As you cover the Technique Lessons, make sure students have a copy of the Practice Test and their answer sheet in front of them. Many of the Technique pages refer to specific questions from the Practice Test.

Ten Days to the ITBS® Suggested Syllabus

Have students take the Practice Test in their books, filling in answers on the bubble sheets. After administering the test, help students correct their tests and fill out the Student Diagnostic Chart (SDC). Collect completed SDCs so you can compile information on the Class Diagnostic Chart (CDC).

DAY	TEN DAYS LESSONS TO USE
1	Administer the *Ten Days* Practice Test
2	Introduction; Basic Skills (Timing, Process of Elimination, Scratch Paper)
3	Vocabulary, Part I: How to Learn Vocabulary Words; Answering Vocabulary Questions; Figuring Out the Part of Speech of a Vocabulary Word
4	Vocabulary, Part II: Positive and Negative Words; Guessing Figurative Meanings; Synonym and Antonym Practice
5	Vocabulary, Part III: Tips to Remember; Practice Questions
6	Reading Comprehension, Part I: Reading Actively; Practice in Active Reading; Tips for Reading Passages; How to Read a Poem
7	Reading Comprehension, Part II: Answering the Questions; Vocabulary in Context Questions
8	Reading Comprehension, Part III: Figurative Language Questions; Specific Information Questions; Emotion Questions
9	Reading Comprehension, Part IV: Drawing Conclusions Questions; Main Idea Questions
10	Review and Exercises: Review any lessons that students had particular difficulties with; complete Practice Passages and finish any remaining exercises.

Teacher's Guide to Diagnostic Charts

Student and Class Diagnostic Charts are included for the Reading Comprehension section of the Practice Test. A diagnostic chart is not included for the Vocabulary section, since it has little variation in question type. However, in the *Ten Days to the ITBS®* teacher wrap, you will find general techniques on how to prepare students for the Vocabulary section on pages 58 to 66.

The Student Diagnostic Chart will give you an accurate account of each student's strengths and weaknesses on the ITBS®. Provide each student with a photocopy of both pages of the chart. Across from each item number, the student will find a blank space. In this blank space, students should mark a *Y* if they answered the item correctly, or an *N* if they didn't. Collect the pages afterward, and use them to evaluate your students' needs.

The Class Diagnostic Chart will help you determine how your class performed as a whole. Once you have collected all the Student Diagnostic Charts, fill in your students' names in the blank spaces provided in the Class Diagnostic Chart, and write the total number of questions students got right in each category. Skimming through the completed chart will give you an excellent overview of the areas you should emphasize during the *Ten Days to the ITBS®* Technique Lessons.

Question Types

There are eight main categories of Reading Comprehension questions. The first six categories are discussed in depth in the Technique Lessons. The last two types, Structure and Author's Strategies, are discussed on page 84 of the Teacher Edition.

- **Vocabulary in Context** questions ask students to define the *meaning of words* that appear in a passage.

- **Figurative Language** questions test students' abilities to make sense of words used metaphorically.

- **Specific Information** questions test students' abilities to retrieve and comprehend *details* in a passage.

- **Emotion** questions ask students about how characters *feel* and what *motivates* their actions.

- **Drawing Conclusions** questions test students' abilities to make *generalizations* based on facts in a passage.

- **Main Idea** questions ask students to identify the *overall theme* of a passage or the author's purpose in writing it.

- **Structure** questions ask students how information in the passage has been *organized* or *developed*.

- **Author's Strategies** questions ask students to determine the author's reasons for including particular sections or phrases or making stylistic choices.

READING COMPREHENSION QUESTIONS

QUESTION	ANSWER	VOCABULARY IN CONTEXT (3)	FIGURATIVE LANGUAGE (4)	SPECIFIC INFORMATION (11)	EMOTION (3)	DRAWING CONCLUSIONS (14)	MAIN IDEA (4)	STRUCTURE (2)	AUTHOR'S STRATEGIES (3)
1	C					■			
2	L					■			
3	B								
4	J			■					
5	D	■							
6	L					■			
7	B						■		
8	L			■					
9	D								
10	L					■			
11	A			■					
12	K								
13	D				■			■	
14	K			■			■		
15	D			■					
16	J		■						
17	D			■					
18	J				■	■			
19	C					■			
20	M					■			

STUDENT DIAGNOSTIC CHART

READING COMPREHENSION QUESTIONS

QUESTION	ANSWER	VOCABULARY IN CONTEXT (3)	FIGURATIVE LANGUAGE (4)	SPECIFIC INFORMATION (11)	EMOTION (3)	DRAWING CONCLUSIONS (14)	MAIN IDEA (4)	STRUCTURE (2)	AUTHOR'S STRATEGIES (3)
21	B					X			
22	L						X		
23	A					X			
24	K					X			
25	D		X						
26	K			X					
27	C				X				
28	J		X						
29	C								X
30	J								X
31	D			X					
32	K			X					
33	A		X						
34	J			X					
35	C								X
36	J			X					
37	D							X	
38	L					X			
39	C					X			
40	K					X			
41	C	X							
42	K					X			
43	C					X			
44	J	X							

CLASS DIAGNOSTIC CHART

READING COMPREHENSION QUESTIONS

STUDENT NAME	VOCABULARY IN CONTEXT (3)	FIGURATIVE LANGUAGE (4)	SPECIFIC INFORMATION (11)	EMOTION (3)	DRAWING CONCLUSIONS (14)	MAIN IDEA (4)	STRUCTURE (2)	AUTHOR'S STRATEGIES (3)

Name: _____ **Date:** _____

Test Section: _____

1 Ⓐ Ⓑ Ⓒ Ⓓ Ⓔ	16 Ⓙ Ⓚ Ⓛ Ⓜ Ⓝ	31 Ⓐ Ⓑ Ⓒ Ⓓ Ⓔ	46 Ⓙ Ⓚ Ⓛ Ⓜ Ⓝ
2 Ⓙ Ⓚ Ⓛ Ⓜ Ⓝ	17 Ⓐ Ⓑ Ⓒ Ⓓ Ⓔ	32 Ⓙ Ⓚ Ⓛ Ⓜ Ⓝ	47 Ⓐ Ⓑ Ⓒ Ⓓ Ⓔ
3 Ⓐ Ⓑ Ⓒ Ⓓ Ⓔ	18 Ⓙ Ⓚ Ⓛ Ⓜ Ⓝ	33 Ⓐ Ⓑ Ⓒ Ⓓ Ⓔ	48 Ⓙ Ⓚ Ⓛ Ⓜ Ⓝ
4 Ⓙ Ⓚ Ⓛ Ⓜ Ⓝ	19 Ⓐ Ⓑ Ⓒ Ⓓ Ⓔ	34 Ⓙ Ⓚ Ⓛ Ⓜ Ⓝ	49 Ⓐ Ⓑ Ⓒ Ⓓ Ⓔ
5 Ⓐ Ⓑ Ⓒ Ⓓ Ⓔ	20 Ⓙ Ⓚ Ⓛ Ⓜ Ⓝ	35 Ⓐ Ⓑ Ⓒ Ⓓ Ⓔ	50 Ⓙ Ⓚ Ⓛ Ⓜ Ⓝ
6 Ⓙ Ⓚ Ⓛ Ⓜ Ⓝ	21 Ⓐ Ⓑ Ⓒ Ⓓ Ⓔ	36 Ⓙ Ⓚ Ⓛ Ⓜ Ⓝ	51 Ⓐ Ⓑ Ⓒ Ⓓ Ⓔ
7 Ⓐ Ⓑ Ⓒ Ⓓ Ⓔ	22 Ⓙ Ⓚ Ⓛ Ⓜ Ⓝ	37 Ⓐ Ⓑ Ⓒ Ⓓ Ⓔ	52 Ⓙ Ⓚ Ⓛ Ⓜ Ⓝ
8 Ⓙ Ⓚ Ⓛ Ⓜ Ⓝ	23 Ⓐ Ⓑ Ⓒ Ⓓ Ⓔ	38 Ⓙ Ⓚ Ⓛ Ⓜ Ⓝ	53 Ⓐ Ⓑ Ⓒ Ⓓ Ⓔ
9 Ⓐ Ⓑ Ⓒ Ⓓ Ⓔ	24 Ⓙ Ⓚ Ⓛ Ⓜ Ⓝ	39 Ⓐ Ⓑ Ⓒ Ⓓ Ⓔ	54 Ⓙ Ⓚ Ⓛ Ⓜ Ⓝ
10 Ⓙ Ⓚ Ⓛ Ⓜ Ⓝ	25 Ⓐ Ⓑ Ⓒ Ⓓ Ⓔ	40 Ⓙ Ⓚ Ⓛ Ⓜ Ⓝ	55 Ⓐ Ⓑ Ⓒ Ⓓ Ⓔ
11 Ⓐ Ⓑ Ⓒ Ⓓ Ⓔ	26 Ⓙ Ⓚ Ⓛ Ⓜ Ⓝ	41 Ⓐ Ⓑ Ⓒ Ⓓ Ⓔ	56 Ⓙ Ⓚ Ⓛ Ⓜ Ⓝ
12 Ⓙ Ⓚ Ⓛ Ⓜ Ⓝ	27 Ⓐ Ⓑ Ⓒ Ⓓ Ⓔ	42 Ⓙ Ⓚ Ⓛ Ⓜ Ⓝ	57 Ⓐ Ⓑ Ⓒ Ⓓ Ⓔ
13 Ⓐ Ⓑ Ⓒ Ⓓ Ⓔ	28 Ⓙ Ⓚ Ⓛ Ⓜ Ⓝ	43 Ⓐ Ⓑ Ⓒ Ⓓ Ⓔ	58 Ⓙ Ⓚ Ⓛ Ⓜ Ⓝ
14 Ⓙ Ⓚ Ⓛ Ⓜ Ⓝ	29 Ⓐ Ⓑ Ⓒ Ⓓ Ⓔ	44 Ⓙ Ⓚ Ⓛ Ⓜ Ⓝ	59 Ⓐ Ⓑ Ⓒ Ⓓ Ⓔ
15 Ⓐ Ⓑ Ⓒ Ⓓ Ⓔ	30 Ⓙ Ⓚ Ⓛ Ⓜ Ⓝ	45 Ⓐ Ⓑ Ⓒ Ⓓ Ⓔ	60 Ⓙ Ⓚ Ⓛ Ⓜ Ⓝ

✂ -

Name: _____ **Date:** _____

Test Section: _____

1 Ⓐ Ⓑ Ⓒ Ⓓ Ⓔ	16 Ⓙ Ⓚ Ⓛ Ⓜ Ⓝ	31 Ⓐ Ⓑ Ⓒ Ⓓ Ⓔ	46 Ⓙ Ⓚ Ⓛ Ⓜ Ⓝ
2 Ⓙ Ⓚ Ⓛ Ⓜ Ⓝ	17 Ⓐ Ⓑ Ⓒ Ⓓ Ⓔ	32 Ⓙ Ⓚ Ⓛ Ⓜ Ⓝ	47 Ⓐ Ⓑ Ⓒ Ⓓ Ⓔ
3 Ⓐ Ⓑ Ⓒ Ⓓ Ⓔ	18 Ⓙ Ⓚ Ⓛ Ⓜ Ⓝ	33 Ⓐ Ⓑ Ⓒ Ⓓ Ⓔ	48 Ⓙ Ⓚ Ⓛ Ⓜ Ⓝ
4 Ⓙ Ⓚ Ⓛ Ⓜ Ⓝ	19 Ⓐ Ⓑ Ⓒ Ⓓ Ⓔ	34 Ⓙ Ⓚ Ⓛ Ⓜ Ⓝ	49 Ⓐ Ⓑ Ⓒ Ⓓ Ⓔ
5 Ⓐ Ⓑ Ⓒ Ⓓ Ⓔ	20 Ⓙ Ⓚ Ⓛ Ⓜ Ⓝ	35 Ⓐ Ⓑ Ⓒ Ⓓ Ⓔ	50 Ⓙ Ⓚ Ⓛ Ⓜ Ⓝ
6 Ⓙ Ⓚ Ⓛ Ⓜ Ⓝ	21 Ⓐ Ⓑ Ⓒ Ⓓ Ⓔ	36 Ⓙ Ⓚ Ⓛ Ⓜ Ⓝ	51 Ⓐ Ⓑ Ⓒ Ⓓ Ⓔ
7 Ⓐ Ⓑ Ⓒ Ⓓ Ⓔ	22 Ⓙ Ⓚ Ⓛ Ⓜ Ⓝ	37 Ⓐ Ⓑ Ⓒ Ⓓ Ⓔ	52 Ⓙ Ⓚ Ⓛ Ⓜ Ⓝ
8 Ⓙ Ⓚ Ⓛ Ⓜ Ⓝ	23 Ⓐ Ⓑ Ⓒ Ⓓ Ⓔ	38 Ⓙ Ⓚ Ⓛ Ⓜ Ⓝ	53 Ⓐ Ⓑ Ⓒ Ⓓ Ⓔ
9 Ⓐ Ⓑ Ⓒ Ⓓ Ⓔ	24 Ⓙ Ⓚ Ⓛ Ⓜ Ⓝ	39 Ⓐ Ⓑ Ⓒ Ⓓ Ⓔ	54 Ⓙ Ⓚ Ⓛ Ⓜ Ⓝ
10 Ⓙ Ⓚ Ⓛ Ⓜ Ⓝ	25 Ⓐ Ⓑ Ⓒ Ⓓ Ⓔ	40 Ⓙ Ⓚ Ⓛ Ⓜ Ⓝ	55 Ⓐ Ⓑ Ⓒ Ⓓ Ⓔ
11 Ⓐ Ⓑ Ⓒ Ⓓ Ⓔ	26 Ⓙ Ⓚ Ⓛ Ⓜ Ⓝ	41 Ⓐ Ⓑ Ⓒ Ⓓ Ⓔ	56 Ⓙ Ⓚ Ⓛ Ⓜ Ⓝ
12 Ⓙ Ⓚ Ⓛ Ⓜ Ⓝ	27 Ⓐ Ⓑ Ⓒ Ⓓ Ⓔ	42 Ⓙ Ⓚ Ⓛ Ⓜ Ⓝ	57 Ⓐ Ⓑ Ⓒ Ⓓ Ⓔ
13 Ⓐ Ⓑ Ⓒ Ⓓ Ⓔ	28 Ⓙ Ⓚ Ⓛ Ⓜ Ⓝ	43 Ⓐ Ⓑ Ⓒ Ⓓ Ⓔ	58 Ⓙ Ⓚ Ⓛ Ⓜ Ⓝ
14 Ⓙ Ⓚ Ⓛ Ⓜ Ⓝ	29 Ⓐ Ⓑ Ⓒ Ⓓ Ⓔ	44 Ⓙ Ⓚ Ⓛ Ⓜ Ⓝ	59 Ⓐ Ⓑ Ⓒ Ⓓ Ⓔ
15 Ⓐ Ⓑ Ⓒ Ⓓ Ⓔ	30 Ⓙ Ⓚ Ⓛ Ⓜ Ⓝ	45 Ⓐ Ⓑ Ⓒ Ⓓ Ⓔ	60 Ⓙ Ⓚ Ⓛ Ⓜ Ⓝ

ITBS® Preparation and Practice

▼▼▼▼▼▼▼▼

DIRECTIONS

This is a test about words and their meanings.

■ For each question, you are to decide which one of the four answers has most nearly the same meaning as the underlined word above it.

■ Then, on your answer sheet, find the row of answer spaces numbered the same as the question. Fill in the answer space that has the same letter as the answer you picked.

1 To **reprimand** the dog
- A comfort
- **B** scold
- C avoid
- D bathe

2 His **discourteous** behavior
- J gentle
- K noble
- L odd
- **M** rude

> Dis- means *not*.

3 The **evidence** to prove her correct
- **A** facts
- B witness
- C statement
- D belief

4 To **yield** the argument
- J oppose
- **K** give up
- L weaken
- M start

> Think of *yielding* to traffic.

5 The **fabricated** story
- A informative
- B well-told
- **C** made-up
- D detailed

> Think of the literal meaning of *fabric*.

6 To **mystify** his fans
- J praise
- **K** confuse
- L lead
- M encourage

> *Mystify* is similar to *mystery*.

7 He walked into the **thicket**.
- **A** bushes
- B cave
- C desert
- D valley

8 The **oral** presentation
- J final
- **K** spoken
- L illustrated
- M written

9 The <u>astute</u> comment

A loud
B funny
C boastful
(D) smart

10 She swept up the <u>shards</u>.

J shredded papers
(K) sharp fragments
L specks of dust
M clumps of dirt

11 To <u>brand</u> as a traitor

(A) mark
B arrest
C criticize
D suspect

> Think of the literal meaning of *brand*.

12 The <u>horde</u> of cattle

J skin
(K) group
L food
M type

13 A <u>resourceful</u> scientist

A curious
B careless
C wealthy
(D) clever

> *Resourceful = full of resources*

14 To <u>detonate</u> fireworks

J prepare
(K) explode
L purchase
M cheer

15 A <u>bizarre</u> story

A long
(B) strange
C silly
D new

16 His <u>aptitude</u> for history

(J) ability
K feelings
L readings
M report

17 Her <u>debut</u> as a musician

A natural talent
B role
(C) first performance
D early education

> *Debut* is French for *beginning*.

18 To <u>mar</u> the tabletop

J polish
(K) damage
L lift
M paint

19 <u>Scant</u> food in the refrigerator

(A) little
B old
C smelly
D tasteless

20 To <u>spurn</u> his offer

J copy
K force
(L) refuse
M fulfill

DIRECTIONS

This is a test of how well you understand what you read.

■ This test consists of reading passages followed by questions.

■ Read each passage and then answer the questions.

■ Four answers are given for each question. You are to choose the answer that you think is better than the others.

■ Then, on your answer sheet, find the row of answer spaces numbered the same as the question. Fill in the answer space for the best answer.

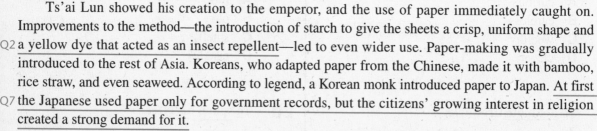

Paper, one of the most important inventions of all time, completely changed the world. It was created in China about 100 B.C., but it took another two hundred years for someone to develop a usable form of it for writing—and many more centuries for the rest of the world to catch up.

An official of the Chinese imperial court, Ts'ai Lun, discovered
Q1 that tree bark, plants, rags, and old fishnets could be turned into paper. He soaked all the ingredients in water to soften and break down the fibers, then mashed them into a pulp. By stretching a piece of cloth
Q9 across a square bamboo frame, Ts'ai Lun made a drying rack similar to a window screen. Using the rack, he scooped up some of the wet slurry and spread it across the stretched cloth. Dried by the hot sun, the slurry turned into a dry, stiff sheet of paper.

Ts'ai Lun showed his creation to the emperor, and the use of paper immediately caught on. Improvements to the method—the introduction of starch to give the sheets a crisp, uniform shape and
Q2 a yellow dye that acted as an insect repellent—led to even wider use. Paper-making was gradually introduced to the rest of Asia. Koreans, who adapted paper from the Chinese, made it with bamboo, rice straw, and even seaweed. According to legend, a Korean monk introduced paper to Japan. At first
Q7 the Japanese used paper only for government records, but the citizens' growing interest in religion created a strong demand for it.

About four hundred years after the Chinese, the Mayans of Central America created their version of paper with fig tree bark. The Aztecs refined the process and became so dazzled by paper that it became a part of religious rituals. Paper arrived in Europe much later. In 751 A.D., during a battle on
Q3 the far western border of China, Chinese craftsmen were taken prisoner and forced to produce paper. Their handiwork reached Europe and eventually spread to the rest of the world.

1 According to the passage, which item was turned into paper by the Chinese?

A Bamboo
B Seaweed
C Rice
(D) Rags

The first three items were used by Koreans.

2 Why did the Chinese add dye to paper?

J It was easier to write on colored paper.
K Religious ceremonies required dye.
(L) Dye helped protect the paper from bugs.
M Dye helped the paper to keep its shape.

3 The paper that first reached Europe came from

A the Chinese emperor.
B the Aztecs.
C a Korean monk.
(D) Chinese prisoners.

4 In the second paragraph, what does "slurry" mean?

J Mud
(K) Liquid mixture
L Dirty water
M Tree bark

See description that precedes mention of *slurry*.

5 How did the emperor probably feel about Ts'ai Lun's paper?

A He wanted only the Chinese to have it.
(B) He thought it was a good idea.
C He wanted it for fishnets.
D He thought it was too hard to make.

6 In the last paragraph, "dazzled by paper" suggests that the Aztecs were

J overwhelmed by its brightness. distractor
K unsure of how to make it.
(L) impressed by its usefulness.
M attracted to its colorful patterns. distractor

Example of figurative language.

7 Why did Japanese production of paper increase?

(A) There was a demand for religious texts.
B The government found new uses for it.
C Average citizens could now write letters.
D The Japanese sold paper to Korea.

8 What seems to be the author's aim in this passage?

J To provide details about the life of Ts'ai Lun
K To explain how paper spread in Asia
L To tell about the independent discovery by the Mayans
(M) To show the way paper evolved into a worldwide product

Avoid choices that refer to just part of text.

9 Which of these is most like the tool used in making paper?

A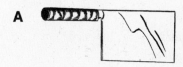

B

C

(D)

DIRECTIONS

This test will show how well you can spell.

■ Many of the questions in this test contain mistakes in spelling. Some do not have any mistakes at all.

■ You should look for mistakes in spelling.

■ When you find a mistake, fill in the answer space on your answer sheet that has the same letter as the **line** containing the mistake.

■ If there is no mistake, fill in the last answer space.

1 (A) suport   *support*
   B infection
   C interest
   D display
   E (No mistakes)

2 J spine
   K recess
   L current
   (M) civilisation   *civilization*
   N (No mistakes)

3 A clench
   (B) alligatar   *alligator*
   C altogether
   D epic
   E (No mistakes)

4 (J) burry   *bury*
   K present
   L genes
   M organ
   N (No mistakes)

5 A arch
   (B) vizion   *vision*
   C programmer
   D length
   E (No mistakes)

6 J symbol
   K instinct
   (L) challenge   *challenge*
   M chipped
   N (No mistakes)

7 A physical
   B inherit
   C glide
   D humid
   (E) (No mistakes)

8 J tusk
   (K) depost   *deposit*
   L contrast
   M survive
   N (No mistakes)

9
- Ⓐ cieling   *ceiling*
- B fourth
- C bare
- D heal
- E *(No mistakes)*

10
- J groan
- K idle
- L whistle
- Ⓜ corse   *coarse* or *course*
- N *(No mistakes)*

11
- A foreign
- Ⓑ equipement   *equipment*
- C aide
- D thief
- E *(No mistakes)*

12
- J withdrawn
- K preacher
- L contend
- Ⓜ raned   *rained*
- N *(No mistakes)*

13
- A camera
- B stormy
- C decent
- D release
- Ⓔ *(No mistakes)*

14
- J pressure
- K unjust
- L quiet
- Ⓜ magishan   *magician*
- N *(No mistakes)*

15
- A imply
- B linger
- Ⓒ abcence   *absence*
- D scream
- E *(No mistakes)*

16
- J atlas
- K foil
- Ⓛ barrle   *barrel*
- M indent
- N *(No mistakes)*

17
- A sleepy
- Ⓑ holor   *holler*
- C identical
- D exaggerate
- E *(No mistakes)*

18
- J plague
- K reserve
- L calculate
- Ⓜ spliting   *splitting*
- N *(No mistakes)*

19
- Ⓐ concieve   *conceive*
- B pictured
- C fractured
- D washing
- E *(No mistakes)*

20
- J logic
- K vital
- L related
- M misuse
- Ⓝ *(No mistakes)*

DIRECTIONS

This is a test on capitalization. It will show how well you can use capital letters in sentences.

■ You should look for mistakes in capitalization in the sentences on this test.

■ When you find a mistake, fill in the answer space on your answer sheet that has the same letter as the **line** containing the mistake.

■ Some sentences do not have any mistakes at all. If there is no mistake, fill in the last answer space.

1
A I bought a new jazz album
(B) for uncle George, who
C will be thirty-seven years old next week.
D *(No mistakes)*
Capitalize *uncle* when followed by proper name.

2
J If you want to rent a Charlie
K Chaplin movie, I think Night Owl
(L) video is still open.
M *(No mistakes)*
Capitalize names of businesses.

3
(A) We went to the beach on the fourth of
B July, launched model rockets from
C Point Lobos, and had a picnic.
D *(No mistakes)*
Capitalize names of holidays.

4
(J) After reading *Turning points in history,*
K I decided to learn more about Roosevelt
L and the Great Depression.
M *(No mistakes)*
Capitalize all main words in titles.

5
A Before becoming an astronaut,
B Judith Resnick worked for Xerox
C Corporation as an engineer.
(D) *(No mistakes)*

6
(J) Catherine the great, who ruled
K Russia in the 1700s, was one of
L Europe's most famous monarchs.
M *(No mistakes)*
Capitalize titles of people.

7
A The National Council of Music
(B) teachers is sponsoring two prizes
C in piano performance.
D *(No mistakes)*
Capitalize names of organizations.

8
J I visited New York City and
K went to the Metropolitan Museum
(L) of Art on fifth avenue.
M *(No mistakes)*
Capitalize street names.

9
A Almost everyone has heard
B of the great deeds performed
(C) by mother Teresa in India.
D *(No mistakes)*
Capitalize titles of people.

10
J Lake Erie is one of the
(K) most important Lakes in
L the Northern Hemisphere.
M *(No mistakes)*
Lakes is not a proper noun; use lower case.

DIRECTIONS

This is a test on punctuation. It will show how well you can use periods, question marks, commas, and other kinds of punctuation marks.

- You should look for mistakes in punctuation in the sentences on this test.

- When you find a mistake, fill in the answer space on your answer sheet that has the same letter as the **line** containing the mistake.

- Some sentences do not have any mistakes at all. If there is no mistake, fill in the last answer space.

1
A   Although Cindy was not a farmer,
B   she grew some of the biggest
(C) potato's anyone had ever seen.
D   *(No mistakes)*
No apostrophe used in plurals.

2
(J) Things Fall Apart was
K   written by Nigerian
L   novelist Chinua Achebe.
M   *(No mistakes)*
Underline or italicize book titles.

3
(A) At the beginning of the trip.
B   my father listened to the baseball game
C   on the radio. We all slept.
D   *(No mistakes)*
Comma needed after introductory phrase; otherwise, it's a sentence fragment.

4
J   "Having never been to Syria,"
(K) said the teacher, I had absolutely no
L   idea what to expect."
M   *(No mistakes)*
Use quotation mark before direct quotation.

5
A   Eggplant is a large oval vegetable.
B   It is closely related to the potato and
C   requires a warm climate to grow.
(D) *(No mistakes)*

6
J   Great Britain refers in part to the
K   three countries found on one large island:
(L) England Wales, and Scotland.
M   *(No mistakes)*
Comma needed after first item in a series of three.

7
A   Moorish architecture dating back
B   to the Middle Ages can be found
(C) throughout Spain, and Portugal.
D   *(No mistakes)*
No comma needed with only two items in series.

8
J   Vespucci explored the coastline
(K) of a large land mass, that turned out
L   to be an unexplored continent.
M   *(No mistakes)*
No comma needed before restrictive clause.

9
A   "Do not be surprised if someday I
(B) run for office" boasted young Michael,
C   who never lacked confidence.
D   *(No mistakes)*
Comma needed after *office*.

10
J   Emily Dickinson, a famous poet
K   of the nineteenth century, was
(L) born in Amherst Massachusetts.
M   *(No mistakes)*
Comma needed between city and state.

DIRECTIONS

This is a test on the use of words. It will show how well you can use words according to the standards of correctly written English.

■ You should look for mistakes in the sentences on this test.

■ When you find a mistake, fill in the answer space on your answer sheet that has the same letter as the **line** containing the mistake.

■ Some sentences do not have any mistakes at all. If there is no mistake, fill in the last answer space.

1
A   While at the ceremony,
(B) Senator Doyle meet the citizens
C   visiting from his hometown.
D   *(No mistakes)*
Use past tense form *met.*

2
J   In Boston, the subway
K   lines are identified by a color
L   code: red, blue, green, etc.
(M) *(No mistakes)*

3
A   Near the tip of Africa is the Cape
B   of Good Hope, an area known for
(C) it's rock formations and bad storms.
D   *(No mistakes)*
The possessive of *it* is *its. It's* is a contraction of *it is.*

4
J   Gotham Restaurant serves desserts
K   shaped like sculpture. You can find
(L) them nowheres else in the city.
M   *(No mistakes)*
Nowhere is the standard form.

5
(A) After she retired next year, Aunt
B   Benita will go to New Mexico
C   for the balloon race.
D   *(No mistakes)*
With first conditional, first verb should be in present tense.

6
(J) When the clock striked
K   one, a tiny cuckoo came out and
L   began to sing merrily.
M   *(No mistakes)*
Correct past tense form is *struck.*

7
A   Twenty percent of the land in
B   Costa Rica has been set aside for parks.
C   Ecology is important to the people there.
(D) *(No mistakes)*

8
J   When she first moved into
(K) Somerville, she didn't know nobody
L   there. It took time to make friends.
M   *(No mistakes)*
Avoid double negatives. Correct form is *anybody.*

9
A   Habitat for Humanity is an
B   organization that specializes in
(C) building new houses to the poor.
D   *(No mistakes)*
Correct preposition is *for.*

10
J   The children took along
(K) there jackets to the football game,
L   since it was cold for October.
M   *(No mistakes)*
The possessive form of *they* is *their.*

This is Part 2 of the test about the use of words. It will show how well you can express ideas correctly and effectively.

Directions: Use this paragraph to answer questions 11–16.

---

1 In preparation for any musical concert, sound engineers must carry out a "soundcheck." **2** Before this soundcheck even takes place, the sound engineer must make sure that all audio equipment is positioned correctly and connected, and to set the microphones up. **3** Then the engineer tests each microphone, as well as the loudspeakers in the concert hall. **4** When he has completed this task, the engineer asks the band to sing and play. **5** He checks to see that all the microphones are plugged in. **6** Sound engineers have particular tastes in the music they like. **7** Finally, the engineer fine-tunes the system to adjust the sound quality and volume.

---

11 Which sentence could be added after sentence 1?

A My uncle, who's a sound engineer, lets me go backstage to watch.

(B) This process is necessary to ensure a crisp, clear sound.

C Audience members should give sound engineers more credit.

D Poor sound quality makes it hard for concert-goers to enjoy music.

12 What is the best way to write the underlined part of sentence 2?

J setting the microphones up

K microphones should be set up

(L) that the microphones are set up

M *(No change)*

Needs parallel structure.

13 What is the best way to write the underlined part of sentence 4?

A Since he has completed this task

B Unless he has completed this task

C This task is complete when

(D) *(No change)*

14 Where is the best place for sentence 5?

J Where it is now

(K) Between sentences 2 and 3

L Between sentences 3 and 4

M Between sentences 6 and 7

15 Which sentence does not belong in the paragraph?

A Sentence 1

B Sentence 3

(C) Sentence 6

D Sentence 7

16 Choose the best concluding sentence to add to this paragraph.

J Everyone has a meal after the soundcheck.

K The sound engineer has nothing to do until the concert begins.

L Musicians usually know less about sound systems than the sound engineer.

(M) Now the soundcheck is complete, and the concert can begin.

The paragraph is about the soundcheck, not sound engineers.

DIRECTIONS

This is a test on capitalization. It will show how well you can use capital letters in sentences.

- ■ You should look for mistakes in capitalization in the sentences on this test.

- ■ When you find a mistake, fill in the answer space on your answer sheet that has the same letter as the **line** containing the mistake.

- ■ Some sentences do not have any mistakes at all. If there is no mistake, fill in the last answer space.

1
A   244 Elm Road
Ⓑ   Princeton, Nj 08540
C   September 22, 1999
D   *(No mistakes)*
Capitalize state abbreviations.

2
Ⓙ   dearest Roberta,
K   I am writing this from the
L   the top of the observation car.
M   *(No mistakes)*
Capitalize letter salutations.

3
A   Traveling by rail aboard the
Ⓑ   coast starlight is a great way to
C   see this beautiful country.
D   *(No mistakes)*
Capitalize proper nouns.

4
J   Yesterday we visited a beach and
Ⓚ   explored some Tidal Pools until it
L   was time for dinner.
M   *(No mistakes)*
Tidal pools is not a proper noun.

5
A   I wish you were with us.
Ⓑ   love,   Capitalize
C   *Antonia*   letter
                       closures.
D   *(No mistakes)*

6
J   After visiting the Lake of the
Ⓚ   woods, Petra decided to explore
L   some lakes in the south.
M   *(No mistakes)*
Woods is a proper noun.

7
A   On March 23, 1775,
Ⓑ   Patrick Henry said, "give me
C   liberty, or give me death!"
D   *(No mistakes)*
Capitalize first word of quoted full sentence.

8
J   In 1271, an Italian explorer, Marco
K   Polo, left Venice and journeyed
L   through Asia to China.
Ⓜ   *(No mistakes)*

9
A   You can see a meteorite
B   and a dinosaur skeleton at the
Ⓒ   museum of Natural History.
D   *(No mistakes)*
Capitalize full name of museum.

10
J   A scout, stagecoach driver, and
Ⓚ   town marshall, Wild Bill hickok was
L   known for his courage.
M   *(No mistakes)*
Capitalize all words in a person's name.

11
A   The papers fell into the
B   river, but Clark's map of the
Ⓒ   nile was not ruined.
D   *(No mistakes)*
Capitalize proper noun *Nile*.

12
J   The lowest point in the country
Ⓚ   of holland is actually 6.7 meters
L   below sea level.
M   *(No mistakes)*
Capitalize country names.

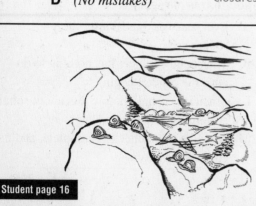

DIRECTIONS

This is a test on punctuation. It will show how well you can use periods, question marks, commas, and other kinds of punctuation marks.

- You should look for mistakes in punctuation in the sentences on this test.

- When you find a mistake, fill in the answer space on your answer sheet that has the same letter as the **line** containing the mistake.

- Some sentences do not have any mistakes at all. If there is no mistake, fill in the last answer space.

1
- **A**   Mr. Wanamaker demanded that
- **B**   his employees be courteous and prompt.
- (**C**) The store opened at nine oclock.
- **D**   *(No mistakes)*

Apostrophe needed in *o'clock.*

2
- **J**   In 1981, a volcano erupted in
- **K**   North America when Mt. Saint
- **L**   Helens exploded in Washington State.
- (**M**) *(No mistakes)*

3
- (**A**)   Beirut the capital of Lebanon
- **B**   is both a port and a center of
- **C**   trade in the Middle East.
- **D**   *(No mistakes)*

Commas needed to set off appositive phrase.

4
- **J**   Babies must be handled very
- (**K**) carefully They have very fragile
- **L**   bodies that can be easily hurt.
- **M**   *(No mistakes)*

Period needed at end of sentence.

5
- **A**   What do you usually eat
- (**B**) for breakfast. I like pancakes,
- **C**   but the rest of my family prefers cereal.
- **D**   *(No mistakes)*

Question mark needed.

6
- **J**   1929 Banton St.
- **K**   Philadelphia, PA 19105
- (**L**)   September 9 1999
- **M**   *(No mistakes)*

Comma needed between day and year.

7
- **A**   Dear Editor:
- (**B**)   Your newspaper says, no more money
- **C**   should be spent on city parks.
- **D**   *(No mistakes)*

No comma needed after *says.*

8
- **J**   Where do you expect kids to
- (**K**) play. The streets are dangerous and full
- **L**   of traffic, and our houses are too small.
- **M**   *(No mistakes)*

Question mark needed.

9
- **A**   I think more money should be spent
- **B**   on parks. If you care about helping
- (**C**) kids keep the parks in good shape.
- **D**   *(No mistakes)*

Comma needed after introductory phrase.

10
- **J**   The entire city will benefit.
- **K**   Sincerely,
- **L**   *Scott Ziff*
- (**M**) *(No mistakes)*

DIRECTIONS

This is a test on the use of words. It will show how well you can use words according to the standards of correctly written English.

■ You should look for mistakes in the sentences on this test.

■ When you find a mistake, fill in the answer space on your answer sheet that has the same letter as the **line** containing the mistake.

■ Some sentences do not have any mistakes at all. If there is no mistake, fill in the last answer space.

1
A   "I want to seize fate
(B) by the throat," say
C   Beethoven in a letter.
D   *(No mistakes)*
Use past tense *said*.

2
J   Mr. Idei, who lives in Tokyo,
(K) flown to San Francisco for the opening
L   of the new entertainment center.
M   *(No mistakes)*
Use past tense *flew*.

3
A   The marching band in the
B   parade was so loud that I
(C) couldn't here Janice talking.
D   *(No mistakes)*
Hear is correct homophone in this context.

4
J   Giant pandas have unique
K   front paws with six fingers. Their wrist
(L) bones have develop extra thumbs.
M   *(No mistakes)*
Use past tense *developed*.

5
A   To teach school children how
B   to read, McGuffy published a series
C   of useful reading primers.
(D) *(No mistakes)*

6
J   Juanita has many clever
K   things to say. She always knows how
(L) to make Ernest and I laugh.
M   *(No mistakes)*
Needs objective pronoun *me*.

7
A   The team was so thirsty that while
B   we played on that hot day, we drank more
(C) than twelve pitcher of ice water.
D   *(No mistakes)*
Needs plural form *pitchers*.

8
J   When you travel in a bus through
(K) Canada, you may spot some mooses
L   on the side of the road.
M   *(No mistakes)*
Correct plural of *moose* is *moose*.

9
A   Jasmine ordered the Halloween
B   costumes by the dozens, knowing that
(C) she couldn't have to many on display.
D   *(No mistakes)*
Too is correct homophone in this context.

10
J   The museum had a special room to
K   display modern inventions that
L   were especially well-designed and creative.
(M) *(No mistakes)*

PART 2 DIRECTIONS

This is Part 2 of the test about the use of words. It will show how well you can express ideas correctly and effectively.

Directions: In questions 11–13, choose the <u>best</u> way to express the idea.

11 A The girl climbed the tree with blue eyes in the backyard. *eyes* modifies *tree*
  B In the backyard with blue eyes the girl climbed the tree. *eyes* modifies *backyard*
  C The girl in the backyard climbed the tree with blue eyes. *eyes* modifies *tree*
  Ⓓ The girl with the blue eyes climbed the tree in the backyard. *eyes* modifies *girl*

12 J In our homes in the future, computers to do even more.
  Ⓚ In the future, computers will do even more in our homes.
  L Computers doing even more in our homes, in the future.
  M In the future, in our homes, computers to do even more.

In (J), (L), and (M), the verb *to do* is not properly conjugated.

13 A To cool it on a rack, Sheila removed it from the oven after baking. vague pronoun reference
  B Removed from the oven, Sheila put the pie, which was done, on a rack to cool. awkward
  C On a rack, after the pie was done, Sheila removed it from the oven to cool. awkward
  Ⓓ When the pie was done, Sheila removed it from the oven to cool on a rack. clear

Directions: In questions 14–16, choose the best way to write the underlined part of the sentence.

14 Although they sometimes worked together, Alexander Hamilton and Thomas Jefferson <u>disagree</u> bitterly over the issue of privilege.
  Ⓙ disagreed   K did not agree   L never agreed   M *(No change)*

15 It will not snow <u>until</u> the temperature drops to 32° F.
  A while   B because   C if   Ⓓ *(No change)*

16 My mother told me that I should stop <u>to sing</u> after 10:00 P.M. to avoid waking my father.
  J because I'm singing   Ⓚ singing   L sing   M *(No change)*

17 Which selection would be most appropriate as a letter of complaint?

A Your toy does not work anymore. It ran for a while, but then it stopped. I also think it should come in a different color. I don't like the color orange. Please tell me what you are going to do about it. unfocused

C Do you think you can cheat little kids? Why do you sell such crummy toys? How come you do not sell good ones that work the way they are supposed to? Please send me one that works right away. too informal

B My mother bought me this toy because I got a good report card. It doesn't work now. I think it should still work, since I still like it. It does not light up now. Please send me another one, and I will send you this one back. contains irrelevant details

Ⓓ I bought a robot two weeks ago and it has stopped working. It is supposed to light up and walk when I press a button, but it no longer does. I put in new batteries, so that is not the problem. Could you please send me a new toy to replace my broken one? brief, focused, and specific

DIRECTIONS

This is a test about using reference materials and libraries.

■ Four answers are given for each question. You should choose the answer you think is better than the others.

■ Then, on your answer sheet, find the row of answer spaces numbered the same as the question. Fill in the answer space for the best answer.

Directions: Questions 1–4 are about using library materials. Choose the best answer for each question.

1 **Where would you look to find a list of recent magazine articles on cloning?**

   A   A science textbook
   B   An encyclopedia
   C   A thesaurus
   Ⓓ   A guide to periodicals

2 **What kind of information would you find in a book's bibliography?**

   J   The date the book was first published
   K   Definitions of key terms that appear in the book
   L   Maps and charts
   Ⓜ   Sources consulted in writing the book

3 **Where would you look to find a synonym for the word *weather*?**

   A   A dictionary
   Ⓑ   A thesaurus
   C   A grammar book
   D   An English textbook

4 **Which of these would probably have the most information about poetry written during the colonial period of American history?**

   Ⓙ   *The Norton Anthology of American Literature*
   K   The "C" volume of an encyclopedia
   L   The index of a history textbook, under "P"
   M   A recent edition of *Who's Who in America*

Directions: This is a portion of the index of a history textbook. Use it to answer questions 5–8.

> **Babylonian Empire,** 61–64
>   Alexander's occupation of, 135
>   calendar, 80
>   social structure, 62
> **Buddhism,** 206–207
>   in China, 226
>   compared to Shinto, 390
>   in Japan, 391

5 **Which page contains information about how Babylonians kept track of the days of the year?**

   A   62   Ⓒ   80
   B   63   D   135

6 **Which page discusses Buddhism as practiced by the Chinese?**

   J   207   L   390
   Ⓚ   226   M   391

7 **Where would you look to find out if Babylonians kept slaves?**

   Ⓐ   62   C   80
   B   65   D   135

8 **Where would you most likely find this index?**

   J   On the first page of the book
   K   After the table of contents
   L   In the middle of the book
   Ⓜ   At the end of the book

An index is almost always found on the last pages of a book.

Directions: Use this page from a dictionary to answer questions 9–14.

ohm (ˈōm) *n.* A unit of measure of electrical resistance.

o·men (ˈō-mən) *n.* An event that predicts the coming of good or evil; a prophetic sign.

om·ni·vore (ˈäm-ni-vōr) *n.* A person or animal that eats both plants and meats.

or·nate (ȯr-ˈnāt) *adj.* **1.** Very heavily ornamented or decorated. **2.** Flowery or showy in style or manner.

or·phan (ˈȯr-fən) *n.* **1.** A child without parents who has not been adopted. **2.** A young animal without a mother. **3.** Someone who lacks support, supervision, or care.

os·cil·late (ˈä-sə-lāt) *v.* **1.** To swing back and forth, usually with a steady rhythm. **2.** To waver, especially between different viewpoints or courses of action; vacillate.

os·prey (ˈäs-prē,-prā) *n., pl.* **ospreys.** **1.** A fish-eating bird with feathers that are dark on the back and white below. **2.** A feather formerly used to trim women's hats.

out·ra·geous (ȧut-ˈrā-jəs) *adj.* **1.** Very offensive to decency or morality; well beyond the bounds of good taste. **2.** To an extreme degree; extravagant, excessive, or immoderate.

9 What is the plural of "osprey"?
A Osprey
(B) Ospreys
C Ospreyes
D Ospreyses

10 In which of the following words is the major accent on the second syllable?
(J) Ornate
K Orphan
L Oscillate
M Osprey

Review phonetic markings with students.

11 Which of the following words would you probably learn about in biology class?
A Ohm
(B) Omnivore
C Ornate
D Outrageous

12 Which of the following might "oscillate," according to the second definition of the word?
(J) A person
K A spring
L A pendulum
M A swing

13 Which word has more than one pronunciation?
A Ornate
B Oscillate
(C) Osprey
D Outrageous

14 In which sentence is the word "ornate" used properly?
J After designing the costume, it was time to *ornate* it. not a verb
(K) John's paintings were all too *ornate* for my taste.
L Although we didn't know it, Karl was an *ornated* speaker. no *-ed* form
M For the holiday, we filled the house with *ornates*. not a noun

ITBS® Practice Test

▼▼▼▼▼▼▼

DIRECTIONS

This is a test about words and their meanings.

■ For each question, you are to decide which one of the four answers has most nearly the same meaning as the underlined word above it.

■ Then, on your answer sheet, find the row of answer spaces numbered the same as the question. Fill in the answer space that has the same letter as the answer you picked.

SAMPLE

S1 To <u>adore</u> the present
   A give
   B love
   C receive
   D return

ANSWER

S1   Ⓐ   ●   Ⓒ   Ⓓ

1 To <u>repel</u> the enemy
A understand
(B) drive off
C fool
D spy on

2 An obvious <u>forgery</u>
J painting
K metal worker
L thief
(M) fake

3 The <u>supreme</u> meal
A large
B heavy
C long
(D) best

4 The <u>minuscule</u> toys
J few
(K) tiny
L light
M scattered

> Think of word *mini*.

5 The <u>vapor</u> in the air
A dust
B sound
C smell
(D) mist

> Term from science class.

6 To <u>shun</u> school work
J complete
K forget
L hate
(M) avoid

7 <u>Conventional</u> approach
(A) accepted
B fresh
C artistic
D legal

> Think *convention*.

8 An obvious <u>asset</u>
J structure
(K) advantage
L decision
M answer

9 She reached the <u>oasis</u>.
A island
B desert
C deep pit
(D) green area

> Term from social studies class.

10 The <u>ogre</u> in the story
(J) monster
K flower
L whale
M vegetable

11 The <u>credible</u> report
A complex
B profitable
(C) believable
D excellent

12 The <u>judicious</u> decision
J significant
(K) wise
L quick
M difficult

> Think *judge*.

13 Her <u>zeal</u> for singing
A voice
B ability
Ⓒ enthusiasm
D training

14 To <u>acquit</u> the person
Ⓙ release
K judge
L accuse
M convict

15 To <u>ascend</u> to the throne
A lead
Ⓑ rise
C be carried
D walk

16 The rule is <u>expansive</u>.
J popular
K well known
L growing
Ⓜ broad

Think *expand.*

17 To <u>trickle</u> the honey
Ⓐ drip
B stir
C swallow
D remove

18 The only <u>peer</u>
J dock
Ⓚ equal
L leader
M student

Note spelling; don't confuse with *pier.*

19 To <u>urge</u> the captain
A salute
B stand beside
Ⓒ press
D restrict

20 The bicycle was <u>audible</u>.
Ⓙ able to be heard
K fixable
L unable to be used
M missing parts

21 Find <u>refuge</u> in the cabin
A peace
B hiding people
C trash
Ⓓ shelter

22 To <u>probe</u> the closet
Ⓙ search
K clean
L push into
M take out of

23 A mysterious <u>hoax</u>
A stranger   neutral
Ⓑ trick
C thief
D box   neutral

Hoax is negative; eliminate neutral answers.

24 The large <u>brood</u>
J loaf
K pitcher
Ⓛ flock
M jacket

25 The actor's <u>quirk</u>
A colorful costume
B large hat
C great talent
Ⓓ odd manner

26 To <u>mediate</u> the discussion
J record
K think about
Ⓛ referee
M conclude

27 To <u>propose</u> a solution
- **A** ask for
- **(B)** suggest
- **C** write down
- **D** create

28 The <u>plea</u> for donations
- **(J)** appeal
- **K** advertisement
- **L** demand
- **M** need

29 <u>Tepid</u> water
- **A** bathing
- **B** unclean
- **C** smelly
- **(D)** warm

30 To <u>linger</u> in the park
- **J** sit
- **(K)** stay
- **L** walk
- **M** play

31 The <u>crest</u> of her career
- **A** achievement
- **B** purpose
- **C** beginning
- **(D)** high point

Think *crest of a wave.*

32 The decision was <u>rash</u>.
- **(J)** unwise
- **K** dangerous
- **L** forgotten
- **M** unusual

33 The <u>dominant</u> player
- **A** back-up
- **(B)** controlling
- **C** oldest
- **D** carefree

Think *dominate.*

34 To <u>scan</u> the horizon
- **J** write about
- **K** paint
- **L** measure
- **(M)** examine

35 To <u>emigrate</u> for freedom
- **A** pass laws
- **B** fight
- **(C)** leave
- **D** sing songs

Contains word *migrate;* implies movement.

36 The town's <u>affluence</u>
- **J** importance
- **K** decline
- **(L)** wealth
- **M** size

37 Built with <u>symmetry</u>
- **(A)** a balanced shape
- **B** a strong material
- **C** a measuring device
- **D** careful planning

38 To <u>compensate</u> for good work
- **J** congratulate
- **K** appreciate
- **L** applaud
- **(M)** pay

39 A <u>vivid</u> portrait
- **A** dim
- **(B)** bright
- **C** old
- **D** new

40 The tool was <u>substandard</u>.
- **(J)** below regular quality
- **K** typical
- **L** useful
- **M** for use underground

Sub = below.

DIRECTIONS

This is a test of how well you understand what you read.

■   This test consists of reading passages followed by questions.

■   Read each passage and then answer the questions.

■   Four answers are given for each question. You are to choose the answer that you think is better than the others.

■   Then, on your answer sheet, find the row of answer spaces numbered the same as the question. Fill in the answer space for the best answer.

SAMPLE

> Susan lay under a sun umbrella, reading a book. She could hear the faint roar of distant waves and the sound of people laughing. Above her head, seagulls flew around in circles, specks of white against the bright blue sky.

S1   **Which of the following places does this passage most likely describe?**

   A   Susan's back lawn
   B   A playground
   C   Susan's living room
   D   The beach

ANSWER

S1   ●

When she was young, Sally Ride never thought she would become America's first woman astronaut. Her interests lay elsewhere, not even in science, but in athletics.

Q2   Sally's parents always encouraged her to do her best. As a youngster, Sally eagerly played baseball and football with the neighborhood boys in Encino, California. Already an accomplished tennis player at the age of eleven, she took lessons from a national women's champion, and after much practice, she became the eighteenth best player on the circuit.

Since she also excelled in her studies, Westlake, a private high school, offered her a scholarship. Sally was an attentive student who breezed through her classes. Coaches noted her abilities as a natural athlete. One gym teacher, in fact, checked Sally's heartbeat after she had run around campus and found that it had hardly risen from the resting rate. Sally seemed destined for a career that combined intelligence and physical endurance.

Sally, however, was a restless student and athlete who yearned to be challenged. She found this challenge in a class in physiology, the study of how the body works. From the moment Sally began studying physiology, she was hooked. The

Q4 subject fascinated her and so did the logical method scientists used to solve problems. She wanted to tackle problems with the same objectivity and independence.

Q1   Even after high school, Sally had not relinquished her dream of becoming a professional tennis player. She even dropped out of college in her sophomore year to improve her tennis skills. After working hard for three months to perfect her game, she came to a major life decision. She realized she would never play well enough to turn professional— or to satisfy herself—so she returned to college.

It was then that she decided to pursue both literature and astronomy, eventually becoming a professor of physics. One day, while reading the campus newspaper, she saw an advertisement placed by NASA to recruit mission specialists for future space flights. Sally knew the job was for her, and eventually she became America's first woman in space.

While orbiting Earth on her first six-day flight aboard the space shuttle, she launched satellites and performed experiments in space. On her next mission, she used a giant remote-controlled arm to launch a satellite that would measure the sun's effect on weather. After spending a few more years with NASA, she left the program to become a space researcher, educator, and children's book writer. She continues to inspire future generations to aim high and reach for their dreams.

1 As a youngster, Ride probably wanted to become

   A a NASA astronaut. not as a child

   B a teacher of science. not as a child

   (C) a pro tennis player.

   D a high school coach.

> Read question carefully; note word *youngster*.

2 How did Ride's parents most likely feel about her interest in science?

   J They wanted her to give up tennis for it.

   K They encouraged her to switch to history.

   (L) They wanted her to work hard at it.

   M They cared more about her athletic ability.

3 In which way was physiology important to Ride?

   A It convinced her to become an astronaut.

   (B) It was the subject that led her to a career in science.

   C It made her read the campus newspaper.

   D It convinced her to leave college for a while.

> Not directly stated; requires inference.

4 According to the text, what aspect of scientific problem-solving fascinated Ride?

   (J) The logic

   K The passion

   L The research

   M The training

5 In the fifth paragraph, what does the word "relinquished" mean?

   A Pursued

   B Begun

   C Thought about

   (D) Given up

> Use context clues to guess meaning.

6 In the sixth paragraph, what is the meaning of the phrase "Sally knew the job was for her"?

   J The job required an interest in literature.

   K The job would make her very famous.

   (L) The job provided challenges to match her skills.

   M The job paid very well.

7 Which of the following best sums up this passage?

   A Ride preferred intellectual interests to all others.

   (B) Ride pursued science, but she could have succeeded in other areas as well.

   C Ride chose a career very early in her life.

   D Ride knew tennis kept her from science, so she quit the game.

> Consult first paragraph for main idea. Eliminate answers that only refer to a part of the text.

(From Accidents May Happen *by Charlotte Foltz Jones)*

You probably push, shove, lean against, sit on, throw stuff on, or look at Masonite many times every day. And you probably don't even realize what it is.

Masonite is hardboard—a pressed wood. You might be sitting on some right now. It's used for drawer bottoms, shelves, door facings, baby furniture, and outdoor signs. A form of it is used to make siding and roofing for houses.

Masonite became Masonite strictly by accident.

Q8 William H. Mason, who had been an associate of Thomas Edison, was probably about fifty years ahead of his time. In 1924 the waste at lumber mills disturbed him. The mills had huge incinerators that burned waste chips, slabs, and edgings.

Paper mills didn't want the waste wood. It contained too much bark. Factories that made insulation board didn't want it. They could get other raw materials and didn't want to bother with "waste" wood. So lumber mills saw no alternative but to burn the wood they couldn't use.

Q10 Mason believed that if he somehow "exploded" the waste wood into tiny fibers, the fibers could be useful. He devised a system: He loaded wood chips into a closed vessel, heated and pressurized the vessel, then jerked open an orifice. The chips exploded into fibers. Mason worked for months to perfect the system.

But there was one problem: What was the stuff good for? Insulation board seemed the only practical use for the "exploded" wood chips.

Then an accident happened.

Q9 One day when Mason went to lunch, he left a fiber mat of the exploded wood chips in a press. It might not have mattered much except that the press had a leaky steam valve, which exposed the fiber mat to both heat and pressure for a long time.

When Mason returned, he found a thin board in place of a thick, soft piece of insulation. The thin board was dense and tough. Mason pounded the new board. He soaked it, cut it, and tested it. The board stood up to every punishment, and Mason realized he had invented something of tremendous value.

But most important to him, he had found a way to use a "waste" product that others thought was useless.

8 What did lumber mills do with scraps?

J   They gave them to Mason.

K   They sent them to paper factories.

(L) They incinerated them.

M   They traded them for raw materials.

9 What was the key factor that led to the successful creation of Masonite?

A   Mason's discovery that he could "explode" wood

B   Mason's collaboration with Edison

C   Mason's decision that wood scraps shouldn't be wasted

(D) Mason's exposure of the fiber mat to heat and pressure

10 The "exploding" of waste wood refers to

J   the result of adding certain chemicals to the process.

K   the last step in the creation of Masonite.

(L) changing it into a more useful form.

M   what happened when water was added.

11 How does the author seem to view Mason?

(A) As a forward-thinking inventor

B   As a bumbling amateur   negative

C   As someone frustrated and slowed by poor equipment   negative

D   As a person who was not methodical   negative

Final paragraph emphasizes how Mason's invention was positive; eliminate negative answers.

12 What appears to be the author's purpose in this passage?

J   To celebrate the benefits of recycling

(K) To tell the story of how a common item was invented

L   To explain how Masonite filled a need

M   To criticize lumber and paper mills

Consult first paragraph to determine author's purpose.

13 How is most of this passage organized?

A   By examining how the accident happened   only one part

B   By showing how Masonite is used to make things   only one part

C   By describing how lumber mills use waste   only one part

(D) By explaining how Mason saw a problem and solved it

Eliminate answers that refer only to parts of the passage.

(From "A Model Family" by Ron Tanner)

All night it rains and hails, clattering on the roof, and this morning everything is glazed with ice—ice on telephone lines, ice on doghouses, ice on bushes and trees, ice on every snowy lawn.

"There are skaters in the street!" says Chip, bounding down the stairs.

"What does it mean?" I ask.

"Breakfast," says Mother from the kitchen.

Q14 Chip slings his ice skates over the back of his chair. "Everything is covered with rock candy." He runs to the bay window in the living room. "This is a special day like in my dreams."

"No school today." I spoon brown sugar over my oatmeal.

"Plenty of time to shovel the driveway," says Mother.

"It's Dad!" says Chip. "It's Dad coming home!"

Mother drops her spoon and hurries to the window. "Where?"

I step between them, leaning on the windowsill. "Some guy skating up the street. It could be anybody, he's so far away."

"He skates just like Dad," says Chip.

"Yes, he does." Mother is squinting. "Sort of."

"Now we can all go skating together."

Mother leans closer to the window. She stands very still, her lips parted slightly as if she's trying to remember something from long ago. "We don't know for sure," she says finally.

"It's him," says Chip. "He's back." He dances around like a leprechaun.

"He would've called," Mother tells us.

"The telephone lines are down," I say.

"Maybe he didn't have a dime," says Chip.

"Where's the telescope," she says. "Get the telescope."

Chip runs into the den and returns with a small, colorfully painted telescope. "From my pirate's chest," he says.

Mother holds the telescope to her right eye and twists the focus ring. The skater is wearing a navy blue overcoat and bell-bottom trousers and a red scarf, which flutters from his neck. He leans from side to side as he pushes forward, skating nearer.

"Is he carrying presents?"

Q17 "Does he have a mustache?" I ask her.

"Or a flat-top haircut?"

"Should we wave?"

"He has a beard," says Mother.

Q18 "He's been away a long time," says Chip.

"He looks unhappy." Mother refocuses.

> Remind students that fictional passages rarely state anything directly. Feelings and thoughts are conveyed indirectly through dialogue, action, and description.

"It's dark and lonely in those little submarines."

"Oh my god, it's Mr. Kiminski."

"Mr. Kiminski!"

Q19 "Old man Kiminski skating this way." She drops the telescope and it hits Chip's left foot. "How can I be so stupid, listening to you kids?" She returns to the kitchen.

14 How does Chip feel about this day?

   J   Annoyed by the storm

   Ⓚ Excited by the weather

   L   Reluctant to see his father

   M Angry with his brother

> Phrase *special day* is a clue.

15 Who is wearing bell-bottom trousers?

   A   The mother

   B   Chip

   C   The father

   Ⓓ Mr. Kiminski

> Identity is revealed only at end.

16 What does Chip mean when he says "Everything is covered with rock candy"?

   Ⓙ He thinks the ice glitters.

   K   He likes brown sugar. distractor

   L   He wants his skates to sparkle.

   M He needs to shovel big ice chunks from the driveway. distractor

> *Rock candy* is used figuratively; eliminate literal interpretations.

17 What might allow the family to identify the father?

   A   A pair of ice skates

   B   A little submarine

   C   A red scarf

   Ⓓ A mustache

18 In this passage, the father has

   Ⓙ not spoken with the family in months.

   K   left the house earlier that morning.

   L   gone on an errand with Mr. Kiminski.

   M returned that afternoon.

19 How does the mother feel in the last paragraph?

   A   Eager to return to the kitchen

   B   Happy to see Mr. Kiminski

   Ⓒ Disappointed in her expectations

   D   Worried about the ice storm

> Question requires inference; mother's clumsiness and anger suggest *hidden* disappointment.

Trees: The Seeds

Q20
{
We are
given light wings,
parachutes, downy legs
that we may be carried aloft
by wind

and drop
where some kind mouse
will bury us in earth;
Q21
{
some squirrel will forget we are food,
leave us

to sprout
green shoots, to weave
rootlets, that we may eat
and drink and grow in time our own
small seeds

—*Myra Cohn Livingston*

Students should read poem at least twice, then jot down a summary sentence. Remind them that the title may help them.

20 In this poem, what are the seeds doing first?

J   Falling on other trees
K   Jumping from tree branches
L   Dropping to the ground
(M) Flying through the air

Make sure students know *we = seeds.*

21 What will happen if the squirrel forgets the seeds are food?

A   The seeds will rot.
(B) The seeds will grow into trees.
C   The squirrel will bury the seeds in the ground.
D   The seeds will be carried by the wind again.

Choice (B) relates to main idea.

22 What is the main topic of this poem?

J   Nature in the forest
K   Animals' influence on seeds
(L) The life cycle of seeds
M   The lightness of seeds

Last three lines suggest main topic.

23 The phrase "grow in time our own/ small seeds" describes

(A) trees reproducing.
B   seeds depending on other seeds for survival.
C   a forest growing.
D   roots producing shoots.

See Q22.

Remind students to read the introductory text. It provides context for the piece.

In thinking about his childhood, Josh recalled the times he spent in his grandmother's kitchen.

It was my grandma's hands that made the bread so good. The gnarled joints and the strong, assured fingers worked the dough in just the right way. She could talk on the phone, and her hands worked by themselves as if she did not need to pay attention to what she was doing. Her fingers pushed, poked, and pressed the spongy ball that would become bread, the Sabbath challah. All challahs included eggs and featured braided dough, but hers was so much

Q25 better than the kind you could buy. Hers arrived every Friday night, a visitor that warmed us, blessed us, and pleased us with its company. Then next week, it appeared again.

She gathered the flour, egg, and water, without a measuring cup in sight. Her trusty wooden spoon, long stained by beet juice and scratched by chicken bones, swirled through the mixture. Dough appeared in the bowl. Then, she balanced the bowl between two burners on top of the stove, suspending it above the white enamel surface. The

Q26 hidden pilot light underneath warmed it, making the dough expand.

I would lift the towel covering the bowl to peek at the beige moon face. Two thumbprints for craters, a palm print for the planes. Later, I would look again, and the moon grew, the craters stretched out. Then my grandma sprinkled flour across the wooden worktable and emptied the dough onto it.

My turn to help her. With her arms moving next to mine, we pushed down making

Q30 handprints—her two large hands circling my two little ones. We snowed more flour on the table. We folded the flattened moon, and pressed down again. Our prints appeared, then disappeared and became part of the challah. Next, the dough rested from our exercising it. By this time, flour covered her, me, and most of the kitchen in fine powder. Now my grandmother divided the dough into four pieces and rolled each into a long log. Then my favorite part arrived. Her fingers danced through the four logs and braided them into a challah. Into the oven it went, and out came the warm, fresh smell of our handiwork.

I couldn't wait for dinner to start. There, at the end of the dining room table, sat the Friday night visitor, golden and shiny. I looked up at my grandma, and she winked. Only

Q29 we knew what it was made of.

24 The author presents his grandmother as

J an expert at making all kinds of bread. no

Ⓚ a competent and loving person.

L a person who was always working. no

M a person who was old and absent-minded. no, she is energetic

> Eliminate statements that are not supported/emphasized.

25 The author compares the challah to

A Grandma's hands.

B the dough.

C a braid.

Ⓓ a visitor.

26 How did the grandmother keep the dough warm?

J By placing it in the oven

Ⓚ By using the heat available from the stove top

L By stirring it with a hot metal spoon

M By kneading it constantly

27 Why did the author help his grandmother?

A To please his parents no evidence

B To learn how to cook perhaps

Ⓒ To spend enjoyable time with her yes

D To have challahs to sell later

no evidence

> Answer must be inferred. Eliminate statements that are not supported/emphasized.

28 In the fourth paragraph, "snowed more flour" suggests

Ⓙ the soft way the flour fell.

K the grandmother's need to finish quickly.

L the iciness of the flour.

M the coldness of the room.

> Interpret phrase based on context. Use the process of elimination.

29 The choice of words in the last sentence helps to emphasize

A the secret baking ingredient in the challah.

B the kneading of the dough.

Ⓒ the love shared by Josh and his grandmother. the wink provides a clue

D flour, egg, and water.

> Interpret phrase figuratively.

30 The phrase "her two large hands circling my two little ones" implies that the grandmother is

Ⓙ guiding Josh.

K correcting Josh's mistakes.

L hurrying to finish.

M warming the dough.

> Consider overall tone of passage when choosing **answer**.

A comet streaks across the night sky with a head of fire and a tail aglow, dazzling us with its silent beauty. It makes an appearance for a few nights or weeks, then retreats for many years.

The fleeting time we can observe the comet represents just a fraction of its life span. Usually, a comet merely floats far away from the sun in a distant zone of space, where the surrounding temperature is more frigid than the chilliest place on Earth. There, it cruises through space about as fast as an automobile speeding down an expressway.

The solid center of the comet, the nucleus, measures from 0.5 to 12.0 miles across—very small in comparison to any of the planets or even Earth's moon. Inside the nucleus exists a frozen mixture of ice and cosmic dust. The sun's ultraviolet light gently bakes the exterior surface until the entire comet is covered with a lumpy crust, both tough and porous.

Occasionally, the sun's faint gravity lures a comet from the distant zone and draws it into orbit. As it approaches the solar heat, the comet's surface warmth increases to an Earth-like room temperature or hotter. The heart of the nucleus, however, remains colder than the North Pole. Now, the sun begins transforming the comet into a giant. At the thinner spots on the crust where the sun's heat can penetrate and reach the ice, geysers of gas and dust erupt like steam from a furiously boiling teapot. The escaping gas and dust generate the spectacular tail we can perceive from Earth. That brew of swirling gases and particles stretches millions of miles long.

As the comet sneaks up on the sun, it starts accelerating until it zooms along at more than 100,000 miles per hour. The brightest portion we see is the coma, or head. Usually, what we perceive as one tail is actually two separate parts: a longer, bluer, and brighter one made of gas, and a shorter, streaked one made of dust. The nucleus that orchestrated the light show, however, remains much too small and dark to be seen—even with a high-magnification telescope.

Remind students to take active reading notes.

31 Where does a comet spend most of its time?

   A It moves across the sky.

   B It travels between Earth and the sun yearly.

   C It hides behind the moon.

   (D) It exists unseen in a very cold part of space.

32 What might ultraviolet light do to a comet?

   J Chill its interior

   (K) Toughen the shell

   L Bring it closer to the sun

   M Send it into the Milky Way

33 In the fifth paragraph, the phrase "the nucleus that orchestrated the light show" means that the nucleus

   (A) generated the tail we can see.

   B caused the comet to expand in size.

   C determined when the comet would appear.

   D controlled the comet's speed.

> Refer to previous sentence to interpret phrase.

34 Which event results in our seeing the comet?

   (J) Dust and gas erupt.

   K The comet's surface hardens.

   L The comet moves toward the sun.

   M The comet warms to Earth's temperature.

35 In this passage, what does the author emphasize about the sun?

   A Its significance in the solar system no

   B Its effect on Earth no

   (C) Its influence on a comet's life

   D Its role in lighting the comet's tail

> Passage is about comet, so emphasis must be on sun's relationship to comet.

36 How has this passage been developed?

   (J) It offers a scientific explanation.

   K It tells the story of one comet. too narrow

   L It describes major space discoveries. no

   M It explains when to best observe comets. too narrow

> Use the process of elimination.

37 What is this passage mostly about?

   A Why comets have tough exteriors no

   B The relationship between comets and planets not mentioned

   C The need for comets in the universe no

   (D) How comets become visible
yes, see first paragraph

38 Which of these is most like a comet when it is farthest from Earth?

   J

   K

   (L)

   M

Blues is a special kind of music that was born at the beginning of the 1900s, evolving from many older African-American musical and cultural elements.

Q39
Work chants sung by slaves in the fields and gospel songs sung by churchgoers were the two most important ingredients that blended together to produce the blues. When these types of music mixed with dance tunes, an early blues style of "call-and-response" emerged. The performer sang a line of a song. Then his guitar would "answer" it with several notes. Renowned blues pioneer Robert Johnson and other early performers appeared alone on stage accompanied by just their guitars, not whole bands. Since no blues records existed yet,

Q40
enthusiastic fans needed to attend live performances to hear Johnson's clever conversations with his guitar.

Many people mistake any sad song for a blues number. The term "blues," however, refers to the playing and singing of special "blue notes." Some historians believe that African-American musicians created the blue sound by "bending" traditional European notes to create off-pitch notes that better matched the African ones they already knew.

Besides the use of special notes, other aspects of a blues performance were distinctive. Johnson and others did not follow the traditional European style of singing, in which a song had an exact length and was presented identically each time. Rather, these skillful performers

Q41
improvised on their songs, based on their feelings and the audience on that particular day. Players of the blues normally performed by themselves, developing such unique styles that they often had difficulties when they accompanied each other.

Q43
Q44
Through the 1920s, blues evolved further to include aspects of jazz and show music. It also grew from a folk art to mass entertainment. In contrast to the early style dominated by men on guitars playing for small audiences, the later classic blues was ruled by female singers with full bands playing on records. Bessie Smith, the greatest of the classic blues singers, was so successful that her records would sell over a half-million copies in just a few months. That is not a high number by today's standards, but it was a great feat back then.

39 Why is blues music considered a "blend"?

A It combined call and response.

B It brought together older and current music.

C It has roots in many different types of music.

D It was sung by slaves and churchgoers alike.

Blend is good key word.

40 What impressed the audiences about Robert Johnson's "clever conversations"?

J His loud singing not mentioned

K His musical skill

L His accomplished band not mentioned

M His easy manner not mentioned

Locate phrase; read entire paragraph it appears in.

41 In the fourth paragraph, what is the meaning of the phrase "improvised on their songs"?

A Memorized their songs

B Asked the audience to sing along

C Added small changes to their songs

D Performed their songs with emotion

42 Why did the early blues singers avoid a European style?

J They could play only certain instruments.

K They preferred the creativity of the blues.

L They could accompany others only with difficulty.

M They wanted to perform show music instead.

Infer from context.

43 According to this passage, how did blues music change through time?

A It was absorbed by jazz.

B It included more female guitar players.

C Its number of fans grew.

D It stopped "bending" traditional European notes.

44 In the final paragraph, what does the expression "mass entertainment" mean?

J Music enjoyed by large numbers of people

K Music that requires many instruments

L Music performed in formal concerts

M Music that combines many forms

Ten Days to the ITBS®

▼▼▼▼▼▼▼▼

Tell your students that the test is like a mystery game. All the clues they need are in the passages they will be reading. The answers will also be in front of them, somewhere in the multiple-choice options. What they have to do is learn how to "play the game" properly in order to arrive at the best answer for each question. *Ten Days to the ITBS®* will show them how to do this.

Introduction

What is the ITBS®?

The ITBS® (which stands for the *Iowa Tests of Basic Skills*) includes sections on reading and language, math, social studies, and science, among other subjects. This book covers only the vocabulary, reading, and language sections.

The ITBS® is a different kind of test. Unlike school exams, the ITBS® is a nationwide test and doesn't correspond with any one school curriculum. Students will most likely encounter new and unfamiliar material, and this may discourage them. Tell them not to get discouraged if they find some questions difficult. They aren't *supposed* to get all the answers right. The good news is that they can learn certain techniques that will increase their chances of making intelligent guesses.

The ITBS® is a multiple-choice test. Explain that multiple-choice tests give students an advantage. The correct answer is right in front of them; they just have to pick it out from three or four wrong answers. This book will familiarize students with the format of the ITBS® and teach special strategies for approaching multiple-choice questions, so they can do their very best.

TEN DAYS TO THE ITBS®

Introduction

What Is the ITBS®?

In the next few weeks, you will be taking a test called the ITBS® (which stands for *Iowa Tests of Basic Skills*). The ITBS® includes tests on reading, vocabulary, math, social studies, and science. Your score on the ITBS® will help your teacher see how well you are doing in these subjects.

In school, you probably take tests regularly. The ITBS®, however, is a little different from the tests your teacher gives in class. This booklet is designed to prepare you for those differences.

When your teacher gives you a test, you usually know the material he or she wants to review. For example, if you've just read *The Old Man and the Sea*, then many questions will probably be about *The Old Man and the Sea*, and you can plan your studies accordingly.

But the ITBS® is different. It includes many topics, and some of the material will be new to you. That's where *Ten Days to the ITBS®* comes in. This booklet tells you what to expect on the ITBS®. It also teaches techniques and valuable tips that will help you do your best on the ITBS®.

Multiple-Choice Tests

First, here's some good news: the ITBS® is a multiple-choice test. That means each question is followed by four or five answer choices. Why is this good news?

> On a multiple-choice test, the correct answer is right in front of you. It is one of the answer choices. You do **not** have to come up with the correct answer entirely on your own. All you have to do is find the correct answer among the answer choices.

ITBS® Test Sections

While this book covers all sections related to language skills, it focuses primarily on the Vocabulary and Reading Comprehension sections.

In the **Vocabulary** section, each word is presented within a short phrase or sentence. Students must choose the closest synonym from the answer choices provided. In the **Reading Comprehension** section, students read seven short passages and answer the multiple-choice questions that follow.

In addition, the *Preparation and Practice* Exercises will give students practice in five other sections related to language. **Spelling, Capitalization,** and **Punctuation** test students' grasp of these basic skills. **Usage and Expression** tests students' knowledge of standard written English and conventions of paragraph organization. **Reference Materials** tests students' ability to use encyclopedias, dictionaries, atlases, and other reference materials, and their knowledge of research strategies.

✊ HELPFUL HINT

This book covers only the sections related to language skills. To find out about the other subjects and to learn what specific battery of tests your students will be taking, speak to the test coordinator in your school.

🍎 TEACHING TIP

You can prepare students for the Reference Materials section in the following ways:

- Assign Exercise 8 (pages 20–21 of the Student Edition) to familiarize students with the format of this section.

- Make sure students feel comfortable using a range of reference materials, such as dictionaries, encyclopedias, atlases, and periodicals.

- Familiarize students with different book sections: the table of contents, index, glossary, and bibliography. Expose students to charts and other methods of presenting information.

- Review basic research skills, and ensure that students know how to use a card catalogue and on-line search engine.

TEN DAYS TO THE ITBS®

ITBS® Test Sections

There are seven sections in the test related to language skills. This booklet concentrates on two of them, **Vocabulary** and **Reading Comprehension**.

1. **Vocabulary:** In the Vocabulary section, each question contains a short phrase with a word underlined. Your job is to find the answer choice that is closest in meaning to the underlined word.

2. **Reading Comprehension:** In the Reading Comprehension section, you will read seven short passages. Each passage will be several paragraphs long, but less than a page. There will be multiple-choice questions after each passage that test how well you understand what you read.

This book will also offer practice exercises for five other sections related to language skills:

3. **Spelling** tests whether you can recognize misspelled words.

4. **Capitalization** tests whether you know how to capitalize words correctly.

5. **Punctuation** tests whether you know how to punctuate sentences correctly.

6. **Usage and Expression** tests your ability to use standard written English.

7. **Reference Materials** tests your ability to conduct research and use reference books, such as the dictionary or encyclopedia.

HELPFUL HINT

To illustrate why students should skip over hard questions, tell them to imagine they are at a party with a piñata. When the piñata breaks, some candy falls in the center of the room, while other pieces roll to hard-to-reach places. To get the most candy, should they go after the easy-to-reach candy or the hard-to-reach candy? Explain that the test questions are like pieces of candy. They are all worth one point, so it makes sense to go for all the easy ones first. Then, if there's time, they can go back and try the harder ones.

TEN DAYS TO THE ITBS®

Basic Skills

 Timing

- For the **Reading Comprehension** section, you will be given 40 minutes to read seven passages and answer 44 questions.
- For the **Vocabulary** section, you will be given 15 minutes to answer 40 questions. (You get more time for the Reading Comprehension section because reading the passages can be time-consuming.)

Take Your Time

Careless mistakes are the most common cause of low test scores. Therefore, you should **never rush through a test**. Rushing causes careless mistakes. It's better to leave out a few questions at the end of the section than to rush.

Take Your Time, But Don't Waste Your Time

Most people don't usually run out of time on tests because they work too slowly. They run out of time because they get stuck on one or two questions. You should try to avoid this common mistake. Here's how:

> If you don't know the answer, either take a guess or skip the question. The time you devote to one difficult question could be better spent answering other, easier questions.

Take your time, but don't waste your time struggling to answer questions that are confusing.

Mark Your Answers Carefully

Always make sure you are marking the correct row on your answer sheet. If you try to work too quickly, you might accidentally mark your answer in the wrong row. For example, if you decide to skip a question on a test, be sure that you also leave that row blank on your answer sheet.

Copyright © by The McGraw-Hill Companies, Inc.

Grade 6/Level 12   PAGE 47   Ten Days to the ITBS®

Basic Skills

· ·

 Timing

For the **Vocabulary section** students will have 15 minutes to answer 40 questions. For the **Reading Comprehension** section students will have 40 minutes to read seven passages and answer 44 questions.

Take Your Time . . .

Emphasize that students should take their time. Rushing through the test can result in unnecessary mistakes. As an example, point out question 19 of the Practice Test, on page 43 (page 35 of the Student Edition). A student skimming this question might not notice that the question refers to the *last paragraph* and might select the wrong answer. Reading *too* quickly leads to silly mistakes.

. . . But Don't Waste Your Time

While students shouldn't rush, they also shouldn't linger on any one question. When students come to a question they cannot answer within a reasonable amount of time, they should skip it and move on to the next question. Suggest that they make a list of the difficult question numbers on the scratch paper, so these skipped questions will be easy to find later on.

How to use the process of elimination to approach questions.

The process of elimination is one of the most important test-taking skills for multiple-choice tests. Introduce this technique early on and review it regularly. By the time the students take the test, this technique should be second nature to them.

Remind students that the great thing about a multiple-choice test is that **the correct answer is always right in front of them.** The downside is that it's hidden amongst the wrong answers. If the wrong answers weren't there, the test would be easy. The process of elimination is a technique to help students get rid of the wrong answers.

To illustrate the usefulness of this technique, have students apply it to the sample question in the Student Edition. Even if they don't know any national holidays in England, they will be able to guess the right answer. Explain that not all the questions will be that easy. However, that's okay. **With every answer choice that is eliminated, the chance of getting the question right improves.** Even if students can only narrow down their choices to just two or three possibilities, they should guess. Educated guessing will improve their test scores.

⛰ SIX STEPS TO THE PROCESS OF ELIMINATION

❶ Write the question number and answer choices on scratch paper.

❷ Read the question.

❸ Read *all* the answer choices.

❹ Cross off any answer choices that are obviously wrong.

❺ If there is only one answer choice left, that's the correct answer.

❻ If there is more than one answer choice left, take a guess.

TEN DAYS TO THE ITBS®

The Process of Elimination

It may sound funny, but it's easier to pick a wrong answer than a right answer—and this will help you! The best way to take a multiple-choice test is to look for **incorrect** answers.

Let's take a look at the question below:

1 **Which day is a national holiday in England?**
A July 4th
B Presidents' Day
C Columbus Day
D Boxing Day

> The ITBS® asks you to pick the best answer from among the choices given. Sometimes the *best* answer is one that doesn't seem to be correct, but you know it's better than the other choices. Eliminate answer choices that are *definitely* incorrect. You'll be surprised how often you will be left with only one remaining answer choice.

Even if you do not know that Boxing Day is a national holiday in England, *you can answer this question* by using the process of elimination! Look at the other answer choices:

- Is July 4th a national holiday in England? Of course not.

- Is Presidents' Day or Columbus Day a national holiday in England? Again, the answer is "No." Both holidays are observed in the United States.

On this question, you can eliminate answers (A), (B), and (C). Only choice (D), Boxing Day, remains. This *must* be the answer.

Sometimes you may be able to eliminate three answer choices. Other times you may only be able to eliminate one or two incorrect answers. That's okay. Even if you can only eliminate one wrong answer, you should still guess from among the remaining answer choices.

> On all but the easiest questions, the process of elimination is the best way to choose an answer.

🍎 TEACHING TIP

To make effective use of scratch paper, students need to write quickly. This skill should be taught, since students tend to write slowly, erasing mistakes as they go.

- Go over concepts of note-taking in class, such as writing in incomplete sentences and crossing out mistakes rather than erasing them. (Use newspaper headlines as an example of condensed writing.)

- Quickly read a passage aloud while students take notes. Have students lay down their pencils shortly after you've finished. Discuss what words different students jotted down. Go over which notes best capture the passage and why.

🔍 How to use scratch paper.

Students are not allowed to write on the test booklet, but they will be provided scratch paper. (Ask your test coordinator if there are any tests for which scratch paper is not provided.) Encourage students to make ample use of scratch paper. Jotting down notes will help them keep track of decisions and organize their thoughts more effectively.

For each question, ask students to write the number and answer choice letters on scratch paper, and then cross out the wrong choices. (The Student Edition provides an illustration of this process.) This method helps students keep track of eliminated answers, and provides a record so it is easier to return and review questions.

Students can also use scratch paper to take notes during the Reading Comprehension section. (Page 67, on Active Reading, describes this process in more detail.)

🍎 TEACHING TIP

When assigning *Preparation and Practice* Exercises, get students in the habit of using scratch paper as a means of taking notes and recording the process of elimination. That way, they will get used to this technique and develop a systematic approach.

TEN DAYS TO THE ITBS®

How to Use Your Scratch Paper

When taking the ITBS®, you will not be permitted to make any marks in your test booklet. However, you *will* be given scratch paper to write on. You might want to use the scratch paper to keep track of answer choices that you know are incorrect, like this:

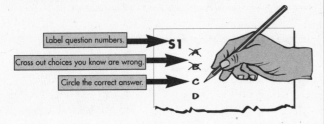

Label question numbers.

Cross out choices you know are wrong.

Circle the correct answer.

If you know that choices (A) and (B) are *incorrect*, draw a line through them on your scratch paper. This way you know that the correct answer must be either choice (C) or (D). On difficult questions, keeping track of wrong answer choices will help you narrow down which one must be correct.

Scratch paper will be most useful in the Reading Comprehension section. As you read a passage, it helps to jot down the main idea of each paragraph and a summary sentence at the end. (See the section on Active Reading, page 59). By creating a "map" of the passage, it will be easier to locate information.

Here's a Hint ➡ Make sure to write quickly and efficiently. Your scratch paper should be clear enough for you to read, but don't worry about writing complete, grammatical sentences. Keep in mind that these notes are for you alone. If you spend too much time on the scratch paper, you might get slowed down.

Grade 6/Level 12

PAGE 49

Ten Days to the ITBS®

Copyright © by The McGraw-Hill Companies, Inc.

Vocabulary Questions

In the Vocabulary section, students will be given 15 minutes to answer 40 questions. Each word is presented within a phrase or sentence, and students are asked to select the best synonym. One way the ITBS® Vocabulary section is unique is that it *seems* to present the words in context, but **the context reveals little about the word's meaning.** All the answer choices will make sense when plugged into the phrase or sentence.

Make students aware of this format, so they will not choose the first answer that seems to "fit." Introduce the concept of context by writing this sentence on the board: *Julia felt so elated that she jumped up and down with joy.* Ask students to guess the meaning of *elated.* (They will probably guess *joyful*, which is correct.) Now ask students to take a look at the two sample questions. Can they guess the meaning of *weary* and *rational*, based on the context? No, they can't.

Explain that this lack of context makes the Vocabulary section somewhat tricky. If the student doesn't know the word's meaning, all the answer choices will seem logical. It's essential to use the process of elimination and review *all* answer choices before selecting one.

EXTRA ACTIVITY

This activity will give your students practice in selecting synonyms. (For another synonym activity, see page 64.)

- Write a list of words on the board that have many synonyms. (Some examples are *happy, sad, walk, eat,* and *look.*) Ask students to brainstorm synonyms of these different words.

- Ask students to focus on one set of synonyms. Which words mean *exactly* the same thing? Which are more distant synonyms? For example, would *saunter* be more similar to *stride* or *tiptoe*? Explain that the ITBS® Vocabulary section will require students to select *exact synonyms.* The more aware they are of slight differences in meaning, the better they will do.

TEN DAYS TO THE ITBS®

Vocabulary Questions

When you take the Vocabulary section of the ITBS®, you will have 15 minutes to do 40 questions. You have to choose the answer choice with the meaning that most closely matches the underlined word.

Let's take a look at the following questions:

> The best way to prepare for the ITBS® Vocabulary section is to study vocabulary. There are no other shortcuts or neat tricks for doing well on this section of the test.

 1 He was <u>weary</u> after the race.
   A tired
   B proud
   C happy
   D lost

 The answer to question 1 is choice (A). *Weary* means *tired.*

 2 She was <u>rational</u> in her thinking.
   J crazy
   K sensible
   L slow
   M creative

 The answer to question 2 is (K). If someone is *rational*, she is *sensible.*

You may have noticed a few things about these questions:

- The phrase in which the vocabulary word appears provides no context clues. In other words, you cannot guess the meaning of the word from the words around it.

- If you didn't know the meaning of the vocabulary word, any of the answer choices could *seem* like the correct answer. You cannot eliminate answer choices simply because they do not seem to fit in the blank.

Since you can't use the context to help you on this section, the best way to prepare yourself is to learn as many words as you can.

Ten Days to the ITBS®   PAGE 50   Grade 6/Level 12

✓ CLASS ACTIVITY

Below are definitions for the words listed in the Student Edition.

❶ *Precipitation* is *hail, mist, rain, sleet, or snow falling to Earth.*

❷ An *oath* is a *solemn vow.*

❸ A *robust* athlete is *strong and energetic.*

❹ A *compulsory* test is *mandatory*—you have to take it.

❺ If you *shirk* a duty, you *avoid* it.

How to learn vocabulary words.

Reading regularly is the best long-term method for building students' vocabularies. Reading a wide variety of materials—books, magazines, Web pages on the Internet, the newspaper—will expose students to many new words. However, even in the short term, students can expand their awareness of vocabulary. The following class activity will help bolster your students' vocabulary skills.

✓ CLASS ACTIVITY

- Divide students into groups of three, and give each group five index cards. The groups should look up each of the five sample words, then write the definition on the front of a card and a sentence using the word on the back. Compare each group's findings.

- Ask students to collect at least five new words a day and write them on index cards. If you want, make this a game. Offer a prize to the student with the largest number of index cards at the end of a week, or to students who find words that nobody else in the class knows the definiton of.

TEN DAYS TO THE ITBS®

How to Learn Vocabulary Words

The best way to learn vocabulary words is to read. The more you read, the better your vocabulary will be. Try the following:

- Start every morning with the newspaper. Any section will do. If you like sports, start with the sports section. If you like theater, start with the arts section. The more you read, the more words you will come across that you don't know.

- You can also increase your vocabulary by reading a wide variety of materials. Books, magazines, the Internet, and even advertisements can all be sources for learning new words.

- Every time you read an unfamiliar word, write it down on an index card. When you have time, look the word up in a dictionary. Write the definition on the other side of your card, along with a sentence using the word correctly. Use the cards to test your vocabulary.

Let's practice. Look up the five underlined words below. Write down each definition on an index card, and then make up a sentence using each word.

1 Heavy <u>precipitation</u> today

2 An <u>oath</u> to her parents

3 The <u>robust</u> athlete

4 A <u>compulsory</u> test

5 To <u>shirk</u> one's duties

Helpful Vocabulary Terms

Synonyms are two different words that mean the same thing. For example: *steal* and *rob; silly* and *foolish; children* and *kids.*

Antonyms are two words that have opposite meanings. For example: *give* and *take; dark* and *light; good* and *bad.*

How to answer Vocabulary questions.

Students should get in the habit of using the process of elimination to approach Vocabulary questions. Use the sample vocabulary question to model this process.

❶ Ask students to cover up the answers with one hand when reading the question stem. Explain that answer choices plant ideas into one's head about what the word means, and these ideas might be wrong.

❷ Ask students to use *perceptive* in a sentence or to define it. For example, they might say *perceptive* means *smart* or *bright*. Don't worry if they don't give the precise definition. Any definition will help narrow the choices.

❸ to ❻ Have students look at each answer choice in order and ask, "Does this word mean the same thing as *smart* or *bright*? If students answer "No," cross the choice out. If students answer "Maybe," put the answer choice aside.

❼ Using this process, students can easily eliminate choices (A) and (B). You will be left with answers (C) and (D). Now ask students to define *perceptive* more precisely. Explain that *perceptive* means you are observant, but not necessarily knowledgeable. Choice (C) is the best answer.

★ EXTRA ACTIVITY

The following activities are fun ways to integrate vocabulary building into classroom lessons.

- Make each Friday Vocabulary Day, in which students are encouraged to use "big words." Award a prize or candy for every challenging vocabulary word that has been used correctly.

- Assign students vocabulary words to look up, define, and act out in a skit, providing enough context for the class to guess the exact definition.

- Give students a list of vocabulary words, and have them incorporate as many as they can in a funny story.

TEN DAYS TO THE ITBS®

Answering Vocabulary Questions

Each question on the Vocabulary section of the ITBS® will give you a phrase with an underlined word and four answer choices. Your goal is to decide which of the answer choices most nearly means the same thing as the underlined word.

Let's take a look at the question below:

1 The **perceptive comment**
   A strange
   B perfect
   C observant
   D knowledgeable

Here's how to approach the question:

1. Read the phrase, but cover the answer choices so you won't be distracted. For example, if you are working quickly, you might select choice (B) because both *perfect* and *perceptive* begin with "per-". Choice (B) is not the right answer. Wrong answers that seem like they might be correct are called *distractors*. Just because two words sound alike does not mean they have similar definitions.

2. If you are familiar with the underlined word, try to think of a word or phrase that means the same thing. For the above example, you might think: *Someone who makes a perceptive comment says something smart.*

3. Now take a look at the answer choices and eliminate the choices you know are wrong. Look at choice (A). Does *strange* mean the same thing as *smart*? No, it doesn't. Get rid of choice (A).

4. Look at choice (B). Does *perfect* mean the same thing as *smart*? No, it doesn't. As mentioned before, choice (B) is a distractor, so you know it is wrong.

5. Look at choice (C). Does *observant* mean the same thing as *smart*? Perhaps. Set aside choice (C).

6. Look at choice (D). Does *knowledgeable* mean the same thing as *smart*? Perhaps. Set aside choice (D).

7. Now consider choices (C) and (D). Both seem close in meaning to *smart*. Which is the better answer? It might help to use *perceptive* in another sentence. You might say: *If you are perceptive, you notice things other people don't.* This quality is clearly different from being *knowledgeable*. Get rid of choice (D). Now you can be certain that (C) is the right answer.

PRACTICE EXERCISE

List some prefixes on the board—*bi-* (two), *bio-* (life), *co-* (with), *im-* and *un-* (not), *mal-* (bad), *dis-* (not)—without revealing their meaning. Have students brainstorm words that contain each prefix, and list these words in a column. After the brainstorming session is complete for each word, ask students to guess the prefix's meaning. Have students look up the prefix in the dictionary and compare the meaning to their guesses.

TEACHING TIP

A more thorough review of common prefixes, suffixes, and root words would be useful in preparing students for the Vocabulary section.

TEN DAYS TO THE ITBS®

Use this technique to try another question:

2   The <u>unwieldy</u> luggage
     J   unattractive
     K   newly purchased
     L   poorly made
     M   awkward

Here's how to approach the question:

1. Read the phrase, covering the answer choices.

2. If you don't know the meaning of the word *unwieldy*, ask yourself if you recognize any part of the word. For example, you might recognize the prefix "un" and know that it means "not." You might also recognize the root word *wield* and be able to use it in a sentence, such as: *He wielded the sword.* You might say that *wield* means something like *hold*. Therefore, you can guess that *unwieldy* means something like *hard to hold*. Keep this phrase in your mind when selecting an answer choice.

3. Uncover the answer choices. Look at choice (J). Does *unattractive* have anything to do with the phrase *hard to hold*? Definitely not. You can get rid of choice (J).

4. Consider choice (K). Does *newly purchased* have anything in common with *hard to hold*? Definitely not. You can get rid of choice (K).

5. Look at choice (L). Does *poorly made* mean *hard to hold* in any way? Perhaps. Put aside choice (L).

6. Look at choice (M). Does *awkward* have anything in common with the phrase *hard to hold*? Yes, it does. Set choice (M) aside.

7. Now you need to choose between choices (L) and (M). It might help to return to the phrase and actually *imagine* a piece of luggage that is hard to hold. You might think of a suitcase that is big or overstuffed. In other words, it is probably *awkward*. Choice (M) is the best answer.

> If you don't know a word, look for clues within the word that might point to its meaning. You might recognize a word contained in another (such as *wield*) or a common prefix (such as "ex-" or "un-"). Other times, you may recognize a word part that appears in another language you have studied, like French or Spanish. Sometimes the clue will help you guess which answer choice is best.

Grade 6/Level 12   **PAGE 53**   Ten Days to the ITBS®

🔍 How to answer Vocabulary questions. (continued)

Even if students can't define a word, they can still make an intelligent guess. If they can recognize any *part* of the word, they can use the process of elimination to arrive at the best answer.

Demonstrate this approach, using the sample question on page 53 of the Student Edition.

❶ Ask students to cover up the answer choices. Tell the class, "Let's try to guess just through our knowledge of parts of the word." If a student knows the definition, tell him/her not to tell the class.

❷ Elicit from the class that the prefix *un-* means *not*. Ask students if they recognize the word *wield*, and if so, to use it in a sentence. They might say, *He wielded a sword.* From this, they can guess that *wield* means *carry* or *hold*. Put this with *un-* and the word might mean something like *hard to hold*.

❸ to ❼ Uncover the choices. Look at each and ask, "Does it have anything in common with the phrase *hard to hold*?" Cross out choices that definitely seem wrong. Students may arrive at (M), the right answer. However, explain that even if they only narrow the choices, they are on the right track.

Figuring Out the Part of Speech of a Vocabulary Word

Words that serve as more than one part of speech can confuse students. For example, the word *stand* has multiple meanings. All students will know the verb form, but fewer will know the noun form in the phrase *to take a stand*. It helps to make students aware of the context of the word in the question—whether it serves as a noun, verb, or modifier—to help them choose an appropriate definition.

Before introducing the sample question, write the word *rule* on the board, and ask students to define it. They will probably come up with more than one definition, based on the noun form (*a rule in school*) and the verb form (*to rule the kingdom*). Now ask students to look at the word as it is presented in the sample question: *To rule the people.* Within this context, can you tell whether *rule* is being used as a noun or a verb? The answer is clearly "Yes." Explain that this is why students should be aware of the part of speech before defining the word. Words change meaning according to how they are used in a sentence.

PRACTICE EXERCISE

- Ask students to brainstorm other words that change in meaning when used as different parts of speech. Some examples you might supply are *record, wax, seal, sound, act, stump, curb, treat, kick,* and *interest.*

- As a follow-up exercise, students can create crossword puzzles based on words with double meanings, and then trade puzzles with a classmate.

- Present a challenge to the class. The student who comes up with the word with the most different definitions wins a prize.

TEN DAYS TO THE ITBS®

Figuring Out the Part of Speech of a Vocabulary Word

Some underlined words serve as more than one part of speech. For example, a word might function as both a noun and a verb, and have different meanings depending on its use. Take the word *stand*. This word can serve as a noun, meaning *a raised platform*. It can also serve as a verb, meaning *to be upright*.

You might be familiar with both meanings. However, if the word appears as a verb in the test and you define it as a noun, you will get confused. For this reason, it helps to determine the word's part of speech. Fortunately, it is easy to tell what part of speech you are reading. It will be a noun, a verb, an adjective, or an adverb.

> To determine the part of speech of a vocabulary word, *look at the answer choices.* All four answer choices will be the same part of speech as the vocabulary word in the question. If all four answer choices are verbs, for example, then the vocabulary word in the question is *also* a verb.

Let's take a look at the following example:

 1 To **rule** the people
  A entertain
  B lead
  C scare
  D classify

 Look at the answer choices. All of the answer choices are verbs. That means that *rule* is also a verb. What does *to rule* mean? If you are still confused, think of a context in which you have heard the word used as a verb: for example, *The king ruled over the land.* Now you should know that the correct answer is (B). To *rule* over a people is to *lead* them, or act as their leader.

Helpful Vocabulary Terms

Noun: A word used for a person, place, or thing, such as *giraffe, father, school,* and *kitchen.*

Verb: A word used for an action, such as *run, jump, hide,* and *write.*

Adjective: A word used to describe a noun, such as *blue, tall, pretty,* and *honest.*

Adverb: A word used to describe a verb, such as *quickly, clearly,* and *carefully.*

FIGURATIVE MEANING EXERCISE

Ask students to brainstorm words that have both literal and figurative meanings. As a starting point, provide the example of the word *cold*. Weather can be *cold*, but an expression can also be *cold*. Divide students into groups and have them generate a list of words that can be used literally or figuratively.

This can lead into a discussion of why people use figurative language and what purpose it serves in writing and spoken expression.

Positive and Negative Words

Even if a student can't remember a word's definition, he or she might sense that the word has a negative or positive connotation. For example, ask your students to look at the sample question. If they have a vague sense that *rebuke* means something negative, this knowledge will help them eliminate answer choices (K), (L), and (M). Obviously, not all questions are as straightforward as this example. However, remind students that if they can eliminate *any* answer choices, this will increase the likelihood of making an intelligent guess.

Guessing Figurative Meanings

Explain to your students that many words have two meanings. The word *shelve*, mentioned in the Student Edition, is one example; other examples are the words *bright, cold, warm,* and *thirsty*. Sometimes the ITBS® will take a word with a common literal meaning and use it figuratively in a way that makes it seem unfamiliar. Knowing the literal meaning can help students guess the answer. For example, in the sample question, knowing the literal meaning of *shoulder* helps one guess the figurative meaning, to *assume* a responsibility.

TEN DAYS TO THE ITBS®

Positive and Negative Words

Even if you aren't sure what a word means, you probably know *something* about it. You might know, for example, whether its meaning is positive or negative. This is useful information! If the underlined word is *positive*, you can rule out all *negative* answer choices. If the underlined word is *negative*, you can rule out all *positive* answer choices.

Let's take a look at an example:

2 To <u>rebuke</u> the neighbor
   J criticize
   K adore
   L help
   M befriend

Suppose you only know that *rebuke* sounds negative. Choices (K), (L), and (M) are all positive. You can eliminate all of them. Choice (J) must be right.

Guessing Figurative Meanings

While taking the ITBS®, you may find yourself at times confused by a word that *seems* familiar but that is used in an unfamiliar way. Some of these words, you will find, are being used in their *figurative* meanings rather than their *literal* meanings.

Take, for example, the word *shelf*. You know a *shelf* is used to store books. *Shelf* also has a verb form. If you *shelve* a book, you put it on the shelf. The verb *shelve* has yet another, figurative meaning. If you *shelve* a plan, you do not put it physically aside. Rather, you simply postpone it. It is *like* shelving a book but not *exactly* the same. Knowing the meaning of one helps you determine the meaning of the other.

Let's take a look at the following example:

1 To <u>shoulder</u> many responsibilities
   A assign
   B avoid
   C understand
   D assume

You know the noun form of *shoulder*. You can also probably assume that the verb *shoulder* means *carry on one's shoulders*. Therefore, if you *shoulder* responsibilities in the figurative sense, you probably *take on* or *assume* them. Choice (D) is the best answer.

Grade 6/Level 12   **PAGE 55**   Ten Days to the ITBS®

Give students practice in selecting synonyms and antonyms.

The ITBS® Vocabulary section requires students to select a synonym for each underlined word. For this reason, students will greatly benefit from practice in pairing synonyms and antonyms.

Review the difference in meaning between *synonym* and *antonym*. Ask students to work in pairs and draw lines connecting the groups of synonyms and antonyms. They can use a dictionary if necessary. (Remind them to write sentences and definitions on index cards for all unfamiliar words.)

Keep in mind that you can use these exercises to continue your discussion of words with double meanings, since many of these words (*order, fume, bend*) have another meaning your students might be more familiar with.

Synonyms:

- **Group 1:** hardy/durable; engulf/overwhelm; brutal/cruel; decree/order.

- **Group 2:** smolder/fume; essence/core; kink/bend; presume/assume.

Antonyms:

- **Group 1:** discord/harmony; generous/stingy; magnify/reduce; entice/repel.

- **Group 2:** movement/rest; perforate/join; stunted/tall; drench/dry.

★ EXTRA ACTIVITY

- Divide students into five teams. Write a word on the board, and give the class one minute to generate synonyms for this word. (*Smile, eat, say, pretty, ugly,* and *friendly* are some good words to use.)

- After one minute, have one group read aloud its list of words. If any other group has the same word, *everyone* has to cross this word out. Repeat this process with the other groups.

- After all teams have shared their lists, they should count up their remaining words and tally their scores; each correct synonym gets one point.

- Play several rounds, and reward the winning team with a prize.

TEN DAYS TO THE ITBS®

Synonym Practice

Synonyms are words that mean the same thing. The ability to recognize synonyms will help you on the Vocabulary section, since correct answers are synonyms for the underlined word in the question. In each group of words below, draw a line connecting the word on the left to its synonym on the right.

Group 1	
hardy	overwhelm
engulf	order
brutal	durable
decree	cruel

Group 2	
smolder	assume
essence	bend
kink	core
presume	fume

Antonym Practice

Antonyms are words that have opposite meanings. Knowing words and their antonyms may come in handy. In each group of words below, draw a line connecting the word on the left to its antonym on the right.

Group 1	
discord	repel
generous	reduce
magnify	stingy
entice	harmony

Group 2	
movement	join
perforate	dry
stunted	rest
drench	tall

Ten Days to the ITBS®

PAGE 56

Grade 6/Level 12

LOOKING FOR VOCABULARY CLUES

Review the methods for finding "clues" in vocabulary words:

- Look for root words.
- Identify prefixes and/or suffixes.
- Decide the part of speech of the word.
- Try to determine positive or negative connotations.
- Identify words with figurative meanings.

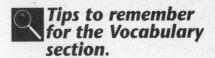 ## Tips to remember for the Vocabulary section.

On the following page, you will find fourteen practice vocabulary questions. Before assigning these questions, review the following points listed in the Student Edition:

- **Take your time.**
- **Don't get bogged down by one or two difficult questions.**
- **Don't finish early.**

Remind students that they will probably encounter many words they don't know. Instead of panicking, they should skip these difficult questions, writing the question number on their scratch paper so they can find it quickly later. They should answer all the easier questions first. Pacing themselves will maximize the number of questions they get right.

- **Define the vocabulary word in your mind.**
- **Read all answer choices first.**
- **Use the process of elimination.**
- **Look for clues in the word.**

Remind students to cover up the answer choices and define the word before looking at the answer choices. If the word is unfamiliar, tell them to use the different strategies listed in the gray box above to narrow their choices. They will come closer to guessing correctly even if they eliminate just one answer.

TEN DAYS TO THE ITBS®

Tips to Remember for the Vocabulary Section

 Take your time. Rushing causes careless mistakes.

 Don't get bogged down by one or two difficult questions. If you get stuck on a question, just skip it and move on.

 Don't finish early. Many students rush to finish even though the test allows them enough time to read carefully. If you get through all the problems before your time is up, go back and review your work.

 Define the vocabulary word in your mind before looking at the answer choices. Doing this will keep you from being distracted by the wrong answer choices.

 Read all the answer choices before choosing your answer. You may find a better answer if you read on.

 If you can't easily determine which answer is correct, use the process of elimination to get rid of incorrect answers.

 Look for clues within the vocabulary words. Figure out the part of speech of each word. Try to determine whether the word has a positive or negative connotation. Think about foreign language words, and consider whether this English word has a foreign language root. All of these techniques will help you eliminate incorrect answers and make good educated guesses.

Be a Word Detective!

Grade 6/Level 12 PAGE 57 Ten Days to the ITBS®

Practice Questions

Directions: For each question, decide which one of the four answers has most nearly the same meaning as the underlined word above it.

1 A <u>candid</u> story
A poetic
B common
(C) frank
D complicated

2 The detective's <u>diligence</u>
J office
K disguise
L schooling
(M) hard work

3 The <u>grandeur</u> of the building
A builder
B use
(C) splendor
D history

> *Grand* in *grandeur* is a clue.

4 The <u>infamous</u> mayor
J well-known
(K) scandalous
L popular
M shy

> *In = not.* Eliminate choices (J) and (L).

5 The <u>enhanced</u> luggage
A attractive
(B) improved
C smaller
D light

6 Enough <u>stamina</u> for the trip
J food
(K) strength
L money
M time

7 A <u>leaden</u> box
(A) heavy
B precious
C rusting
D weak

> *Lead* is a metal that is heavy.

8 The <u>meager</u> selection
J colorful
(K) small
L new
M additional

9 The <u>glutton</u> finished the meal.
A cook
B customer
(C) overeater
D guest

> A *glut* is too much of something.

10 To <u>flaunt</u> the prize
(J) show off
K win
L purchase
M compete for

11 He was in <u>peril</u>.
A shock
B love
(C) danger
D disbelief

12 To <u>cavort</u> with friends
J travel
(K) play
L race
M explore

13 To <u>rebuff</u> the idea
(A) reject
B develop
C think of
D forget

> Remind students that answer choices that resemble the underlined word are not necessarily distractors. Here, *reject* is right.

14 The <u>stoic</u> traveler
(J) patient
K celebrated
L adventurous
M efficient

SIX STEPS TO READING ACTIVELY

❶ Use your scratch paper to write down the title or subject of the passage.

❷ Read the first paragraph.

❸ On the scratch paper, number that paragraph.

❹ Write one or two phrases summarizing the paragraph.

❺ Repeat Steps 3 and 4 for each paragraph.

❻ At the end, write a brief, one-sentence summary of the entire passage.

TEN DAYS TO THE ITBS®

Reading Comprehension

When you take the Reading Comprehension section of the ITBS®, you will have 40 minutes to read seven passages and answer 44 questions. The passages vary in length from a half-page to a full page. They may be fiction or nonfiction.

It is important to read the passages carefully. Don't forget, however, that you have to answer questions to earn points toward your final score! Don't linger over the passage. Remember that you can (and should) go back to the passage to look for answers.

Don't Try to Memorize the Passage

Some students think that they should try to remember every word of the passage as they read. Don't make this mistake! It is impossible to remember *everything* in a passage.

It is also unnecessary to remember every detail. The passage will still be in your test booklet when it is time to answer the questions. You can look at it to find the information you need *whenever you want to!*

Read Actively!

When you read a passage for the first time, your goals should be to:

- identify the main idea of the passage.
- get a rough idea of where different facts are located in the passage.

The best way to accomplish these goals is to read the passage actively. Here are some ways to read actively:

- Use your scratch paper to take notes. After reading each paragraph, briefly jot down a sentence or phrase.

- When you finish reading a passage, stop for a moment and ask yourself, "What did I just read about?" Write a brief sentence summarizing the main idea of the passage.

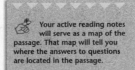 Your active reading notes will serve as a map of the passage. That map will tell you where the answers to questions are located in the passage.

Copyright © by The McGraw-Hill Companies, Inc.

Grade 6/Level 12   PAGE 59   Ten Days to the ITBS®

Reading Comprehension

In the Reading Comprehension section of the ITBS®, students will have 40 minutes to read seven passages and answer 44 questions. The following Technique Lessons will introduce different types of passages and questions and explain the best strategies for answering the questions.

Don't Try to Memorize the Passage

When approaching a passage on a test, students often read slowly, trying to memorize facts. There is no point in doing this on the ITBS®, since they can return to the text while answering the questions. Rather, students should get a sense of the *structure* of the passage, so they know where to find information. Explain that a passage is like a library; it has all the information you need, so long as you know where to look.

Read Actively!

As students read, they should use scratch paper to jot down summary sentences after each paragraph and at the end. This process is called **active reading**. In doing so, students will create a kind of "map" of the passage that will help them locate specific information, make inferences, and understand the author's strategies for organizing the material.

The More You Read, The Better You'll Do!

The best way to prepare students for the Reading Comprehension section is to expose them to a wide variety of reading material. The more familiar they are with a variety of genres—biographies, poetry, fiction, essays, as well as practical forms of writing, such as letters and advertisements—the better they will do. Frequent reading assignments, especially those combined with writing activities and class discussion, will make students more confident and perceptive readers.

HELPFUL READING COMPREHENSION TERMS

- **Passage:** The text you read before answering questions.

- **Main Idea:** What a passage or paragraph is mainly about.

- **Theme:** An idea raised by or discussed in the passage.

- **Summary:** A brief statement of main points covered in a passage.

- **Setting:** The time period and place in which a passage happens.

- **Figurative Language:** Language which describes one thing in terms of something else.

TEACHING TIP

On page 61 of the Student Edition, students will get a chance to practice active reading. Before introducing this activity, make sure to review the concept of the *main idea* of a passage.

Tell a brief story or read a short passage aloud, and then ask students to write a summary sentence. You can also use newspaper headlines to introduce this concept, since headlines are essentially condensed main idea statements.

For more discussion of how to identify the main idea, see the Technique Lessons on pages 83–84.

TEN DAYS TO THE ITBS®

Helpful Reading Comprehension Terms

Passage: The text you read before answering questions. It may be a story, a poem, or a group of paragraphs containing factual information.

Main Idea: What a passage or paragraph is mainly about.

Theme: Another word for main idea. Sometimes there is a lesson to be learned from the theme of a story.

Summary: A brief statement of the main points covered in a passage.

Setting: The time period and place in which a passage happens.

Figurative Language: A colorful or creative way of writing, in which one thing is described in terms of something else. Figurative language is especially important in poetry.

The More You Read, the Better You'll Do!

The best way to prepare for the Reading Comprehension section of the test is to read as much as you can. The more you read, the better you will understand *what* you read.

It doesn't matter what you read. Books, magazines, Web pages, newspapers, billboards, and toothpaste tubes are all good. Just make reading a habit, and you'll be on the right track.

TEACHING TIP

Tell students to imagine the following scenario: You are walking to your house with your new friend Ron and he whips out a note pad. Each time he sees a new sight—a shrub, tree, mailbox, street sign—he meticulously records it in his notebook. He explains, "I want to make sure I know the way to your house." What is wrong with Ron's approach?

Explain that Ron is no different from many readers. Some readers feel they must write notes on *every single detail* of the passage. Readers should just take notes on the main idea of each paragraph—not every little fact.

Give students practice in active reading.

Use the blues passage, taken from the Practice Test, to give students practice in active reading.

Tell students to use scratch paper and write a number for each paragraph. They should jot down a summary sentence or phrase after each paragraph and sum up the main idea at the end. Remind students to write general ideas rather than specific facts.

Here are some sample summary sentences:

Paragraph 1: Blues formed from many elements.

Paragraph 2: Blues evolved from work chants and gospel songs. "Call-and-response" style emerged. Performers appeared alone.

Paragraph 3: *Blues* refers to blue notes—"bending" of European notes to match African ones.

Paragraph 4: Blues players improvised, freer than Europeans.

Paragraph 5: 1920s blues became more mainstream; more female singers.

Final summary phrase: Where blues came from/ how it evolved.

TEN DAYS TO THE ITBS®

Practice in Active Reading

Here is a passage from the practice test you just took. Use it to practice reading actively. Take out a piece of scratch paper and number it from 1 to 5, one number for each paragraph. Write a summary sentence or phrase after the corresponding number. When you are finished reading, write the main idea of the passage on your scratch paper in a few words. Make sure to focus on the general idea, not the specific details.

Blues is a special kind of music that was born at the beginning of the 1900s, evolving from many older African-American musical and cultural elements.

Work chants sung by slaves in the fields and gospel songs sung by churchgoers were the two most important ingredients that blended together to produce the blues. When these types of music mixed with dance tunes, an early blues style of "call-and-response" emerged. The performer sang a line of a song. Then his guitar would "answer" it with several notes. Renowned blues pioneer Robert Johnson and other early performers appeared alone on stage accompanied by just their guitars, not whole bands. Since no blues records existed yet, enthusiastic fans needed to attend live performances to hear Johnson's clever conversations with his guitar.

Many people mistake any sad song for a blues number. The term "blues," however, refers to the playing and singing of special "blue notes." Some historians believe that African-American musicians created the blue sound by "bending" traditional European notes to create off-pitch notes that better matched the African ones they already knew.

Besides the use of special notes, other aspects of a blues performance were distinctive. Johnson and others did not follow the traditional European style of singing, in which a song had an exact length and was presented identically each time. Rather, these skillful performers improvised on their songs, based on their feelings and the audience on that particular day. Players of the blues normally performed by themselves, developing such unique styles that they often had difficulties when they accompanied each other.

Through the 1920s, blues evolved further to include aspects of jazz and show music. It also grew from a folk art to mass entertainment. In contrast to the early style dominated by men on guitars playing for small audiences, the later classic blues was ruled by female singers with full bands playing on records. Bessie Smith, the greatest of the classic blues singers, was so successful that her records would sell over a half-million copies in just a few months. That is not a high number by today's standards, but it was a great feat back then.

Different types of Reading Comprehension passages.

The ITBS® contains several types of Reading Comprehension passages. Each requires a slightly different approach, so teach your students to recognize them.

❶ **Fictional Passages** are excerpts from novels or short stories. They are *narrative* in structure and often require students to infer characters' emotions. The main point or message often reveals itself at the end.

❷ **Informational Passages** have an essay form. The first paragraph usually introduces the main idea of the passage, and the following paragraphs develop it.

❸ **Biographical Passages** tell true stories, but they often have a narrative structure and dramatize events through description and dialogue.

❹ **Poems** require students to infer meaning and emotion and to make sense of figurative language.

❺ **Functional Passages** include everyday writing—letters, speeches, advertisements, etc. While there are no functional passages in the Grade 6 ITBS®, they can be found in other levels.

🍎 TEACHING TIP

Students may view biographical texts as merely a list of chronological facts without any central message. Explain that biographies, like any other text, are organized to prove a point. Explain that a biographer could paint almost any subject to be a hero or villain, depending on which details were included or excluded.

Ask students to appraise the Sally Ride passage with this point in mind. What aspects of her personality have been highlighted? What do these selective details reveal about the main point the author is making?

TEN DAYS TO THE ITBS®

Tips for Reading Passages

 Read the passage actively. Active reading will provide you with a map of the passage. This map will help you find the answers to questions.

 Don't try to memorize every detail. Plan to go back to the passage to look for information when you are answering the questions.

 Always read the introductory text that precedes the passage. These few sentences may contain valuable information that will help you understand the passage. There may also be questions that you will understand better if you have read the introduction.

 Note any words that you don't understand. Try to figure out what they mean from the words around them. Even if a question doesn't ask specifically about that word, knowing the word might help you understand another fact or even the main idea.

What Are the Reading Comprehension Passages Like?

There are several different kinds of Reading Comprehension passages on the ITBS®: Fictional, Informational, Biographical, Poetic, and Functional. Here's a description of each:

1. **Fictional Passages** are passages that are made up. They are short stories or parts of novels. On the practice test, the passage about the ice-skater in the street was fictional.

2. **Informational Passages** may seem similar to reading a textbook. They will tell you facts about people, places, or things. On your practice test, the passage about Masonite was informational.

3. **Biographical Passages** are stories about the lives of real people. On your practice test, the passage about Sally Ride was biographical.

4. **Poems** on the ITBS® can be about anything. They will be short, but there will be a lot to look at on each line. The poem on the practice test was "Trees: The Seeds."

5. **Functional Passages** may look like a letter, a speech, or an advertisement. There are often many facts presented in a functional passage.

TEACHING TIP

Many students find poetry intimidating. Tell them not to be discouraged. Explain that poetry works on many different levels, using sound, rhythm, and imagery to convey meaning.

Ask the class if anyone ever heard a new song, liked it, but couldn't fully understand the words at first. Explain that poetry sometimes affects us the same way—we may not understand every word, but we still respond to it emotionally. Tell students to trust their instincts and not to worry if they don't understand every single part of the poem.

How to read a poem.

Poetry can be daunting, since poets rarely state anything directly. For this reason, the more exposure students have to poetry, the better. If time permits, bring a poem to class and discuss it with your students. Conclude the discussion by reviewing basic steps to approaching a poem.

❶ **Read the title.** Tell students that titles are helpful in figuring out the focus of the poem.

❷ **Read the poem slowly and carefully.** Explain that poems are a very condensed form of writing—each word counts.

❸ **Look for figurative language.** This is a central way poets convey meaning. Read the line by Wordsworth: *I wandered lonely as a cloud.* Ask students to brainstorm word associations with this image. Explain how Wordsworth *intended* us to feel all these things. Poems are so rich because each word or phrase evokes many emotions.

❹ **Keep questions in mind while reading the poem.** Ask yourself, "What's happening? How does this poem make me feel?"

❺ **Summarize the main idea, theme, or lesson at the end of the poem.** The main idea can often be found in the last stanza.

TEN DAYS TO THE ITBS®

How to Read a Poem

1. **Read the title or introduction.** Sometimes poems are confusing. The title or introduction may tell you in a straightforward way what the poem is about.

2. **Read the poem slowly and carefully.** There is often a lot of information packed in each line.

3. **Look for figurative language.** The poet William Wordsworth once wrote, "I wandered lonely as a cloud." Wordsworth didn't mean that he was literally a cloud. Rather, he was just using figurative language to compare himself to a cloud.

   Whenever you come across an example of figurative language, try to imagine for yourself what the poet means. As you read Wordsworth's line, for example, you might ask yourself, "How does a cloud move?" Imagine a person moving in the same way. This process of visualizing an image may help you understand Wordsworth's message.

4. **Keep these questions in mind as you read:**
   • What happens in the poem?
   • Where does the poem take place?
   • Who are the characters?
   • What is the mood of the poem? What image are you left with?

5. **Summarize the main idea, theme, or lesson at the end of the poem.**

 Facts and Opinions

When you are reading an ITBS® passage, whether it's a poem or a functional passage, it helps to remember the difference between facts and opinions.

Facts are statements that are always true. Everyone can agree about facts. Here are two examples: "A dollar is worth one hundred pennies"; and "Whales are mammals."

Opinions are personal feelings. People can have different opinions about the same facts. Here are some opinions: "Turnips taste bad"; "I like to go camping"; and "Football is the best sport."

Copyright © by The McGraw-Hill Companies, Inc.

Grade 6/Level 12   PAGE 63   Ten Days to the ITBS®

General strategies for the Reading Comprehension section.

Each passage is followed by a set of questions that test a variety of reading skills.

Answering the Questions

Review these basic tips for answering questions:

- **Read the question carefully.** When students skim a question, they might misunderstand it and choose the wrong answer.

- **Refer back to the passage and your active reading notes.**

- **Use the process of elimination.** Keep track of wrong answers on scratch paper.

- **Don't get stuck on difficult questions.** Mark the number on your scratch paper and return to it later.

- **Use key words to locate information.** (See page 77 for more on key words.)

The Different Types of Reading Comprehension Questions

The Technique Lessons will discuss six main question types found on the Grade 6 ITBS® test: Vocabulary in Context; Figurative Language; Specific Information; Emotion; Drawing Conclusions; and Main Idea.

In addition, the Teacher Edition will discuss two other question types—Structure questions and Author's Strategies questions—that are included on the diagnostic charts but not covered in the Student Edition.

🍎 TEACHING TIP

Present students with the following scenario. Four wrapped boxes are in front of them, and one contains their dream present, whatever that may be. (Elicit some ideas.) They can choose and keep *just one* package. How can they increase their chances of choosing the right one? Have students suggest different strategies for figuring out the contents of a package.

Explain that educated guessing works in the same way. Random guessing is the equivalent of grabbing the first package you see. Educated guessing involves individually judging each package—or each answer choice—and asking, "Is this the one I should pick?"

TEN DAYS TO THE ITBS®

Answering the Questions

After you read each passage, you will answer questions about what you have just read. All the information you need to answer the questions can be found in the passage.

 Here's a Hint → *When You Answer the Questions*

- **Take your time reading each question. Make sure you understand exactly what is being asked.** The wording of some questions may confuse you. Take the time to reread any question if you are not exactly sure what it is asking.

- **Refer back to the passage.** If you've read the passage actively, it should be easy to find the facts you need. Remember that the information you need to answer a question will always be found somewhere in the passage you just read. Use your map to find it!

- **Cross off any answer choices you know are wrong.** Keep track of these choices on your scratch paper. (See page 49 for more information on how to use your scratch paper.)

- **If a question is so hard that you can't even eliminate one answer choice, go on to a different question.** If you have time at the end, return and take a second look. Don't waste time by getting stuck on one tricky question.

The Different Types of Reading Comprehension Questions

Let's take a look at the different kinds of questions that will come up in the Reading Comprehension section. They can be grouped into six broad categories:

1. Vocabulary in Context
2. Figurative Language
3. Specific Information
4. Emotion
5. Drawing Conclusions
6. Main Idea

WATCH OUT FOR WORDS WITH DOUBLE MEANINGS

While Vocabulary in Context questions offer many clues to help students, they also pose certain challenges. Some students may assume that if they know the meaning of a word, they can easily answer the question. For example, they might read the phrase *dwell on* and assume it means *live in*, just because they know *dwell* can mean *live*. Remind them that a single word can have multiple meanings, as discussed on pages 62–63. Students need to determine the *meaning in context* to choose the correct answer.

How to approach Vocabulary in Context questions.

Students *need* a broad vocabulary to do well on the Vocabulary section. In contrast, students can do well on the Vocabulary in Context questions simply by using context clues to guess the meaning. For example, students can read the sentence "The *chivalrous* knight was rewarded for his success on the battlefield" and guess that *chivalrous* has something to do with bravery. Even if they just know it means something positive, this knowledge will help them eliminate answer choices.

In other words, by learning basic guessing strategies, students can greatly improve their performance on these questions.

LET'S TAKE A LOOK AT QUESTION 5 FROM YOUR PRACTICE TEST.

Students can use context clues to guess what *relinquished* means. They know that Sally Ride dropped out of college to play tennis, so at that point she still wanted to become pro. Ask them to fill in the sentence with another word that makes sense, based on the information given. They might say: *Sally had not given up her dream of becoming a professional tennis player.* The answer is (D), *given up*.

TEN DAYS TO THE ITBS®

Vocabulary in Context Questions

Vocabulary in Context questions ask you to define the meaning of words that appear in the passage. There is a good chance that you will *not* recognize these words, because most are fairly difficult. However, all of these words appear in sentences that provide **context clues** to the word's meaning.

Consider this sentence: "The *chivalrous* knight was rewarded for his success on the battlefield." The context clue here is "success on the battlefield." This should tell you that the word *chivalrous* has something to do with bravery.

Even when context clues don't reveal exactly what a word means, they can at least tell you what it *doesn't* mean. Consider the sentence, "She clapped her hands, shrieked with joy, and whirled around in a state of *euphoria*." You can guess just from the context that *euphoria* means something positive. By crossing out negative words from your answer choices, you will come closer to selecting the right answer.

Let's take a look at question 5 from your practice test:

> Even after high school, Sally had not relinquished her dream of becoming a professional tennis player. She even dropped out of college in her sophomore year to improve her tennis skills. After working hard for three months to perfect her game, she came to a major life decision. She realized she would never play well enough to turn professional—or to satisfy herself—so she returned to college.

5   **In the fifth paragraph, what does the word "relinquished" mean?**

    A   Pursued

    B   Begun

    C   Thought about

    D   Given up

If you don't know what *relinquished* means, you could use the context to figure it out. You just read that Sally dropped out of college to play tennis, so you know she had not yet given up her ambition to become a pro. Therefore, you can guess that *relinquish* probably means to *give up*. So, the best answer choice is (D).

Grade 6/Level 12   PAGE 65   Ten Days to the ITBS®

EXERCISES

Have students complete the Vocabulary in Context exercises, then review the answers. Show how each question can be answered through the use of context clues.

QUESTION 1

Have students cover up the answer choices and read the two sentences, leaving a blank space where the word *garish* is. What word would make sense in the blank? *Showy, suspicious,* and *dangerous* might all be possible substitutes. Now look at the answers and eliminate those that don't make sense. Choice (B), *flashy*, is the best answer.

QUESTION 2

Read the first sentence, leaving a blank where *abundant* is. What word would make sense in the blank? If Roosevelt has a gigantic task ahead, he clearly needs lots of energy. Choice (K), *much*, is the best answer.

QUESTION 3

Explain that *however* suggests that an argument is changing direction. The second sentence emphasizes Ling's vast knowledge of fish, so the third sentence probably describes what she *doesn't* know. Choice (B), *puzzle*, is the best synonym for *mystify*.

EXTRA ACTIVITY

Play the Imaginary Word game with your class to reinforce the concept of context clues:

- Divide students into groups of four.

- Tell each group to think of a silly word (the weirder and funnier the better), write a dictionary definition for it, and use the word in a sentence.

- As each group reads its sentence aloud, the rest of the class should try to guess the meaning of the word.

- At the end, the class can vote on the "best" (i.e., funniest) imaginary word.

This game demonstrates that even unfamiliar words can be understood through their context.

TEN DAYS TO THE ITBS®

Exercises

Directions: Read each excerpt and answer the question that follows it.

> The fugitive chose the new clothes carefully. He knew that to hide from the police, he couldn't look garish when walking down the street.

1 In the passage above, the word "garish" probably means
  A poorly dressed.
  B flashy.
  C casual.
  D uncomfortable.

> President Roosevelt's efforts to push the country out of the Great Depression would demand abundant energy. The task that lay ahead was gigantic. The cure was tough, but to veer from this path would certainly have meant an even bigger crisis ahead.

2 In this passage above, the word "abundant" probably means
  J a little.
  K much.
  L mental.
  M political.

> Long before Ling became a famous scientist, she was fascinated by fish. As a very young girl, she could identify many of them. Their ability to breathe underwater, however, continued to mystify her and compelled her to become a scientist.

3 In this passage above, the word "mystify" probably means to
  A bore.
  B puzzle.
  C excite.
  D frustrate.

⧩ FIVE STEPS TO ANSWERING FIGURATIVE LANGUAGE QUESTIONS

❶ Cover up the answer choices so you don't get distracted.

❷ Locate the phrase in the passage, and read the lines before and after to get a sense of the context.

❸ In your head, briefly define what the phrase means. Make sure the definition makes sense when considering the context.

❹ Uncover the answer choices. Use the process of elimination to get rid of clearly wrong answers.

❺ Choose the best answer from those that remain.

⧠ How to approach Figurative Language questions.

Figurative Language questions involve more inference than Vocabulary in Context questions. For this reason, students tend to be intimidated by them. Calm their anxieties by demonstrating how they are already pros at understanding figurative language. Read the following sentences and ask students to interpret them:

- *Susannah ran like a jack rabbit.*

- *Raphael wore a sunny expression.*

- *The fog crept into town on cat's paws.*

This exercise should demonstrate how students already have the tools to make sense of figurative language.

⧗ LET'S TAKE A LOOK AT QUESTION 28 FROM YOUR PRACTICE TEST.

Emphasize that students cannot guess the correct meaning of this phrase without first reading the passage. Here, *snowed* has nothing to do with cold, but with how snow falls. Flour falls the same way—softly and gently. In other words, students should always rely on context when interpreting Figurative Language questions.

TEN DAYS TO THE ITBS®

Figurative Language Questions

A writer uses figurative language to describe one thing in terms of something else. One example would be "John smiled brightly." A smile clearly doesn't *literally* give off light. However, a smile appears to us to be "bright," since it warms us and makes us happy. This is an example of figurative language.

Figurative Language questions are similar to Vocabulary in Context questions. The difference, however, is that Figurative Language questions will often ask you for the meaning of a phrase instead of just a single word. You are most likely to see one or more Figurative Language questions when the passage is a poem.

Let's take a look at question 28 from your practice test:

> My turn to help her. With her arms moving next to mine, we pushed down making handprints—her two large hands circling my two little ones. We snowed more flour on the table. We folded the flattened moon, and pressed down again. Our prints appeared, then disappeared and became part of the challah. Next, the dough rested from our exercising it. By this time, flour covered her, me, and most of the kitchen in fine powder.

28 In the fourth paragraph, "snowed more flour" suggests

    J the soft way the flour fell.

    K the grandmother's need to finish quickly.

    L the iciness of the flour.

    M the coldness of the room.

 As you read this passage, it should become clear that flour is sprinkled on the worktable and then worked into the dough. The flour gently drops from the grandmother's hand, in a way that resembles snow falling. Therefore, the best choice is (J).

> *Five Steps to Answering Figurative Language Questions*
>
> 1. Cover up the answer choices so you don't get distracted.
> 2. Find the place in the passage where the phrase appears. Reread the lines preceding and following the phrase to help understand the context.
> 3. In your head, briefly define what you think the phrase means. Make sure your definition makes sense when considering the context.
> 4. Uncover the answer choices. Use the process of elimination to get rid of answers that are obviously wrong.
> 5. Choose the best answer from the choices that are left.

EXERCISES

Have students complete the Figurative Language exercises, then review the answers. Emphasize the importance of context in answering these questions.

QUESTION 1

According to the text, people in Louisiana like spicy cayenne peppers. Therefore, you can guess that *more fire* means *spicy*. Choice (D) is the best answer.

QUESTION 2

Explain that poems frequently take simple ideas and present them in an unfamiliar way, often using figurative language. What is meant by *fifty springs*? First, students should figure out that *room* is being used figuratively to mean *time*. *Fifty springs* is meant to represent a period of time. The poet is using *springs* to mean *years*. Choice (L), *years*, is the best answer.

QUESTION 3

The paragraph explains that the shark depends on its keen sense of smell. Therefore, the phrase *a nose with fins* is probably the writer's way of emphasizing the importance of the shark's nose. Choice (D) is the best answer.

★ EXTRA ACTIVITY

Introduce the term *simile* and explain how a simile compares two things. A simile often uses the word *like*. Ask students to think of something they love to do. Give students a minute to jot down particular reasons why they like this activity. Then ask them to come up with a simile to describe it, and to explain this simile in a paragraph. The simile should convey this experience as vividly as possible to their classmates. An example might be: *dancing* is *like flying*.

Have students read their paragraphs, and write the similes on the board. Ask students which similes they liked best, and why.

TEN DAYS TO THE ITBS®

Exercises

Directions: Read each excerpt and answer the question that follows it.

> Cayenne peppers are hot stuff. Add a few to a pot of bubbling tomato sauce, and you have a spicy treat ready to light up a pile of shrimp and scallops. In Louisiana, folks prefer their food with more fire than people from up North. But I say, give them a taste, and they'll convert.

1 What does the author mean when he writes that Louisiana "folks prefer their food with more fire"?
A They like their food cooked longer.
B They prefer warmer food.
C They cook with higher flames on the stove.
D They enjoy food with more pepper.

> And since to look at things in bloom
> Fifty springs are little room,
> About the woodlands I will go
> To see the cherry hung with snow.

2 The phrase "fifty springs" refers to
J trees.
K flowers.
L years.
M planting.

> A shark possesses such sensitive hearing that it knows when a wounded fish is thrashing more than a half-mile away. Its sense of smell is even sharper, with the largest part of its brain devoted to smelling prey. In many respects, a shark is a nose with fins, since so much of its life is devoted to finding food.

3 What is meant by the phrase "a nose with fins"?
A The shark looks funny.
B The shark swims by using its nose, in addition to its fins.
C The shark uses only its sense of smell.
D The shark's life depends largely on finding food by smell.

PRACTICE EXERCISE

Have students practice identifying key words or phrases and skimming passages for information. Ask students to look at questions 3, 26, 32, and 34 of the Reading Comprehension section of the Practice Test, and identify the best key word or phrase, if possible. (Tell them there is *one* question with no clear key word.)

Answers:

#3: Key word is *physiology*.

#26: Key word is *dough*.

#32: Key phrase is *ultraviolet light*.

#34: There is no clear key word. Here, students should consult their reading map to find the answer.

How to approach Specific Information questions.

These questions require students to locate and retrieve factual information. Remind students that all the information they need is in the passage; they just need to locate it quickly.

Scan for key words. Choosing a *key word* in the question will help students locate answers in the passage. Explain that key words function like flags, telling you where to find information. For example, if the date 1921 appears in the question, you can easily skim the passage for 1921. The answer will surely be somewhere nearby.

Read actively. Active reading notes will also help students locate information. The more carefully they summarize each paragraph, the faster they will find the information they need. (Notes are especially useful for questions without a clear key word, such as question 34 in the Practice Test.)

LET'S TAKE A LOOK AT QUESTION 8 FROM YOUR PRACTICE TEST.

Ask students to select a good key word or phrase. (*Lumber mills* would work best.) Then ask them to skim the text and find this key phrase. In paragraph 4, they will find that mills "burned waste chips, slabs, and edgings." Choice (L) is correct.

TEN DAYS TO THE ITBS®

Specific Information Questions

Specific Information questions ask you to find details in the passage. Refer back to the passage to find the information needed to answer these questions.

Here are a few things to consider when answering Specific Information questions:

- **The correct answer choice will often be worded a little differently than it appears in the passage.** Don't let that confuse you!

- **You will sometimes need to combine information from different places in the passage to answer a question.** Remember to scan the entire passage for all the details that might apply.

- **Keep an eye out for questions that use the words *except* and *not*.** It is easy to make careless mistakes on these questions.

Let's take a look at question 8 from your practice test:

> William H. Mason, who had been an associate of Thomas Edison, was probably about fifty years ahead of his time. In 1924 the waste at lumber mills disturbed him. The mills had huge incinerators that burned waste chips, slabs, and edgings.

 8   **What did lumber mills do with scraps?**
  J   They gave them to Mason.
  K   They sent them to paper factories.
  L   They incinerated them.
  M   They traded them for raw materials.

To find the answer, go back to the passage. You will see that the author explains that the lumber mills burned the waste wood in incinerators. Therefore, Choice (L) is correct.

Three Steps to Answering Specific Information Questions

1. **Look for a key word or phrase in the question that will help you locate the answer.** For example, in the question above, a good phrase might be *lumber mills*.

2. **Scan the passage for key words.** When you find one, read the section surrounding it and use the information it contains to answer the question. Remember that sometimes you'll have to look at two different parts of the passage to find the answer.

3. **Look at the answer choices and use the process of elimination to identify the best answer.**

Copyright © by The McGraw-Hill Companies, Inc.

Grade 6/Level 12   PAGE 69   Ten Days to the ITBS®

EXERCISES

Assign the exercises on page 70 of the Student Edition, then review the answers. With each question, have students cover up the answer choices, skim the passage for information, and answer the question *in their own words*. Only then should they look at the answer choices.

QUESTION 1

When trying to answer the question in their own words, students might say that Chicago developed a distinctive style because many musicians moved there. Which answer choice best expresses this idea? Cross out (C); musicians played in clubs, not restaurants. Eliminate (B); this sound developed on State Street, not everywhere. (A) is wrong because Chicago didn't *recruit* musicians. The best answer is (D).

QUESTION 2

The passage says that the cemetery was underground, two-thousand years old, and recently discovered when a donkey tripped on an opening to it. Choices (J), (L), and (M) are all wrong or unsupported. Choice (K) is the best answer.

HELPFUL HINT

Remind the students of the following points:

- **The correct answer choice is almost always worded differently than it appears in the passage.** It is a *paraphrase* of the author's words. Make this clear to students; otherwise they may overlook the answer.

- **Sometimes students will have to combine two or more pieces of information from different places in the passage to determine the answer.** Remind them that when they are taking the actual test, they may need to skim the entire passage for relevant details.

TEN DAYS TO THE ITBS®

Exercises

Directions: Read each excerpt and answer the question that follows it.

At night, the State Street area became a popular destination because of its nightclubs, cafés, cabarets, and restaurants. Many musicians traveled from the South to play in the local clubs and contributed to Chicago's distinctive musical style. There was so much talent present in the lively neighborhood that a popular saying claimed that a horn would play itself if it was just held out in the wind.

1 Chicago developed a special musical sound
  A by recruiting musicians from other cities.
  B everywhere in the city.
  C in the State Street restaurants.
  D with the help of players from the South.

Most Egyptian mummies were found by pure chance, not by archeologists gently poking the earth. The Bahariya Oasis was discovered in 1996 by a donkey. The animal stumbled on a dirt road and caught its leg in a hole. That opening led to an underground tomb, which was part of a two-thousand-year-old cemetery.

2 The cemetery at Bahariya Oasis was
  J located in ancient times.
  K unearthed through a donkey's accident.
  L first uncovered by archeologists.
  M found on a desert surface.

🍎 TEACHING TIP

To illustrate the concept of emotional clues, have students reread the passage on page 34 of the Practice Test. Then discuss it as a group: "How does Chip feel at the beginning of this passage? How does the mother feel?" List words or phrases that describe their inner feelings. Then discuss the conclusion of the passage, and ask, "How have their feelings changed? How can we tell?"

🔍 How to approach Emotion questions.

Emotion questions are inferential. They require students to use context clues—what the characters do and say—to infer how they *feel* and what motivates their actions. The passage will usually not explicitly state "John was sad" and then ask directly if John was sad. Students must use **emotional clues** to infer this information.

Explain that students are already experts at interpreting emotional clues. Ask them, "When your friend is having a bad day, how can you tell?" They might mention slumping shoulders or lack of eye contact. Explain that they are drawing conclusions based on emotional clues. As readers, they go through the same process.

Review the four steps to answering Emotion questions listed in the Student Edition, and have students use them when approaching the sample question.

↗️ LET'S TAKE A LOOK AT QUESTION 14 FROM YOUR PRACTICE TEST.

First, have students identify a key word or phrase in the question. They might select *Chip* and how he feels about his *day*. They will find more information in paragraph 5. Chip's comparison of ice to *rock candy* and his statement "This is a special day like in my dreams" both convey positive expectations. Choice (K) is the best answer.

TEN DAYS TO THE ITBS®

Emotion Questions

Emotion questions ask you about how characters feel and what motivates their actions. Sometimes the story will state the answer directly. Other times you will have to look for clues in the passage to figure out the answer.

Let's take a look at question 14 from your practice test:

> "Breakfast," says Mother from the kitchen.
>
> Chip slings his ice skates over the back of his chair. "Everything is covered with rock candy." He runs to the bay window in the living room. "This is a special day like in my dreams."

14 How does Chip feel about this day?
  J   Annoyed by the storm
  K   Excited by the weather
  L   Reluctant to see his father
  M   Angry with his brother

 Chip says this is a "special day like in my dreams" and speaks of the ice as "rock candy," a phrase that suggests something appealing. Therefore, the correct answer is (K).

Four Steps to Answering Emotion Questions

1. **Skim the passage for key words or phrases.** For instance, in the question above, it would help to look for a reference to *Chip* and how he feels about the *day*.

2. **Read the sentences before and after the key words, looking for hints about the character's emotions or reasons for acting a certain way.** Remember, it may not be as simple as "he was excited." The look on a character's face, the dialogue, and even the setting can contain hints about the character's emotions and motivations.

3. **In your own words, write down an answer to the question.**

4. **Look at the answer choices and use the process of elimination.** Pick the answer choice that is closest to what you've written down.

Grade 6/Level 12   PAGE 71   Ten Days to the ITBS®

EXERCISES

Have the students complete the exercises on this page. Emphasize that they should make sure to consider the *whole* passage—not just the sentences around key words—before making a judgment. Some emotional clues can be conflicting, and a detail taken out of context may be misinterpreted.

QUESTION 1

With this question, students need to look for clues about the *author's* emotions. (See the gray box for more on this type of question.) The author describes early planes as *flimsy*, which may suggest that the answer is (A). But the author also speaks of the *daredevil pilots* and how they *challenged their own physical endurance*—phrases that suggest admiration. Choice (B) is the best answer.

QUESTION 2

Marisol's father is *worried* about her interactions with boys. While he seems *strict*, there is no evidence of him being *angry* or *annoyed*. Choice (M) is best answer.

QUESTION 3

The text provides clear emotional clues about how Nawrose feels about chess: he practices several hours a day and plays against a computer to improve his skill. There is no evidence that this enthusiasm is forced. Choice (A) is the best answer.

AUTHOR'S ATTITUDE QUESTIONS

Some Emotion questions ask about the author's attitude toward a topic. Prepare students for this question type by reviewing terms that might appear as authors' attitudes: *neutral, amused, admiring,* and *critical.* Elicit other possible attitudes an author might have toward a subject. Explain that if a text has a *neutral* tone, it is hard to determine the author's personal feelings. If the author offers strong opinions or seems particularly poetic or descriptive, the tone becomes biased—either *admiring* or *critical.*

For further practice, have students bring in newspaper articles and determine whether or not they are biased. Ask them to underline key phrases that suggest bias or slanting.

TEN DAYS TO THE ITBS®

Exercises

Directions: Read each excerpt and answer the question that follows it.

The early years of aviation were dominated by daredevil pilots steering flimsy planes made of wood and canvas. Those aircraft were nothing like today's sleek aluminum jets, which are more like floating cruise ships with every comfort. Back then, many pilots became world famous for their dangerous exploits in the air. They challenged their own physical endurance and the plane's technical limitations.

 1 What seems to be the author's attitude toward the early pilots?
  A Amusement at their simple airplanes
  B Admiration for their skills and daring
  C Curiosity about their ability to fly at all
  D Jealousy of their fame

The class trip to Washington would be so much fun, thought Marisol. She could sit on the bus talking with her best friends on the long ride, and they'd have such a good time staying in a hotel for the two nights. She had saved enough from baby-sitting to pay all the expenses herself. Marisol knew, however, that there was a serious roadblock—her father. He was worried about certain boys in her class, especially after the incident last month.

 2 Which of the following best describes Marisol's father?
  J Excited
  K Annoyed
  L Angry
  M Concerned

Always practicing, Nawrose Farhan Nur became a world chess champion before he turned ten years old. When his family moved from Bangladesh to New York City, he adjusted quickly. After school each day, he completed his homework and then practiced his chess for several hours. Later in the evening, he played against a computer to master complicated moves.

 3 How does Nawrose feel about chess?
  A Dedicated to it
  B Confused by it
  C Somewhat interested by it
  D Forced to play it

Ten Days to the ITBS®   PAGE 72   Grade 6/Level 12

Copyright © by The McGraw-Hill Companies, Inc.

DON'T FORGET

Drawing Conclusions questions never require students to make random guesses. The passage will always provide clues for students to use, even if the answers are not stated directly. Remind students that they are like detectives, using all the available information to make intelligent guesses.

FOR FURTHER PRACTICE

Tell students to refer once again to the fictional passage on page 34 and look for clues that might help them answer question 18. Discuss what reasons the author might have for not explaining where the father is.

How to approach Drawing Conclusions questions.

Drawing Conclusions questions are similar to Emotion ones, only they require students to draw conclusions about facts, not feelings.

Most Drawing Conclusions questions are impossible to identify. They look exactly like Specific Information questions—only the information cannot be found in the text. Students must draw upon their overall understanding of the text to make a logical guess.

Review the four steps listed in the Student Edition, and have students use them when approaching the sample question.

HELPFUL HINT

Students may be tempted to draw conclusions based on their own experience. Warn them that this may be misleading. They should base their conclusions *only* on clues from the text.

LET'S TAKE A LOOK AT QUESTION 42 FROM YOUR PRACTICE TEST.

When locating the answer, students might choose the key phrase *European style*. The text never tells us *why* the blues singers avoided the European style; however, it mentions that the *performers improvised on their songs*. This suggests that they enjoyed freedom of expression. Choice (K) is the best answer.

TEN DAYS TO THE ITBS®

Drawing Conclusions Questions

Drawing Conclusions questions ask you to draw conclusions based on facts in the passage. The answers to these questions are not directly stated in the passage—instead, they are only suggested.

Let's take a look at question 42 from your practice test:

> Besides the use of special notes, other aspects of a blues performance were distinctive. Johnson and others did not follow the traditional European style of singing, in which a song had an exact length and was presented identically each time. Rather, these skillful performers improvised on their songs, based on their feelings and the audience on that particular day. Players of the blues normally performed by themselves, developing such unique styles that they often had difficulties when they accompanied each other.

42 Why did the early blues singers avoid a European style?
- **J** They could play only certain instruments.
- **K** They preferred the creativity of the blues.
- **L** They could accompany others only with difficulty.
- **M** They wanted to perform show music instead.

The passage never states directly *why* blues singers avoided a European style. You have to look for the clues in the passage. The paragraph tells *how* the European and blues styles differ, but that does not explain *why*. The words *improvised on their songs, based on their feelings* does reveal that the blues players created their music based on how they felt. Therefore, the best answer is choice (K).

Four Steps to Answering Drawing Conclusions Questions

1. **Skim the passage for key words.** In the example above, an excellent key word to look for would be *European*.

2. **Reread the paragraph around the key word, and look at your summary sentence of that paragraph.**

3. **Write down what you think the facts in the paragraph suggest.**

4. **Use the process of elimination.** If none of the answer choices matches your conclusions, try to eliminate choices that are not supported by the facts in the passage. Then take your best guess from the remaining choices.

Grade 6/Level 12   PAGE 73   Ten Days to the ITBS®

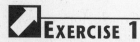
EXERCISES

Have students complete the two exercises on page 74 of the Student Edition. Ask them to underline clues that helped them answer each question.

EXERCISE 1

Students should look for clues about why the uncle is training Charles. The uncle, described as a *strict educator*, quizzes Charles about his knowledge of nature and tells him to look carefully at everything he sees. Choices (A), (B) and (D) can be dismissed for lack of evidence; they *may* be true, but there is no supporting evidence in the passage. Choice (C) is the most precise answer.

EXERCISE 2

With this passage, students will need to read all the answer choices before returning to the paragraph. Which of the choices can they eliminate, based on the text? It appears that these friends are serious star-watchers—they own telescopes and know how to chart a star's position—so students can cross out (K). There is no evidence to support (L) or (M), so these choices can also be eliminated. Choice (J) is the best answer.

★ EXTRA ACTIVITY

For extra credit homework, tell one student to imagine a crime scenario, write a paragraph describing it, and then list items or clues that a detective might find at the scene of the crime. The next day, have the student present these clues to the class. Tell the class to use this evidence to reconstruct the crime. Discuss possible options for around twenty minutes; then tell the student to reveal the actual scenario.

This activity is a fun way to demonstrate the process of drawing conclusions. As a follow-up discussion, have students distinguish between educated guesses and wild guesses, and discuss how they can avoid wild guesses as a reader.

TEN DAYS TO THE ITBS®

Exercises

Directions: Read each excerpt and answer the question that follows it.

> Charles's training as a young brave came from his uncle, a strict educator. "Look closely at everything you see," his uncle would tell him as he left the teepee each morning. When Charles returned, his uncle often asked him questions about what he had seen—the different colors of bark on a tree, the proper names of all the birds nearby, the reason fish gathered at a particular place in the lake, and much more.
>
> "You ought to follow the example of the wolf," Charles's uncle would say. "Even when he is surprised and runs for his life, he will pause to take one more look at you before he enters his final retreat. So you must take a second look at everything you see."

1 What is Charles's uncle's main purpose in this passage?
A To teach Charles how to retreat like a wolf
B To tell Charles the tribe's legends about nature
C To show Charles how to be a good observer and scientist
D To act as Charles's parent

> The friends drove one hundred miles from Phoenix into the desert to escape the light pollution. A mile down a dirt road off the main highway, they set up their three telescopes, ready to look at the night sky. After midnight, one noticed a faint glow to the south he couldn't identify. Another charted its position to see if it moved. They had discovered something important.

2 The friends probably
J are very serious amateur astronomers.
K have not observed the stars before.
L enjoy astronomy because they hate city life.
M will set up their telescopes in Phoenix next time.

THREE STEPS TO ANSWERING MAIN IDEA QUESTIONS

Review the following steps with your students.

❶ **Read actively.** Remind students that their summary phrases should include only general ideas, not specific details.

❷ **Reread the title and introductory blurb, if there is one.** Reread the first and last paragraphs. Remind students that essays often state the main idea in the first and last paragraphs, and poems and stories often reveal the meaning at the end.

❸ **Use the process of elimination.** Be systematic about choosing answers. In general, avoid choices that are overly specific or overly general.

How to approach Main Idea questions.

Main Idea questions ask students to assess the passage as a whole and to identify the main point it is making. Some ask directly for the main idea; others ask students to identify the author's purpose.

Remind students that in Main Idea questions, they should **consider the passage as a whole**. Some of the answer choices may *seem* right because they mention facts discussed in a single paragraph of the passage. For instance, in question 37 of the practice test, choice (A) may seem tempting, since the passage discusses the exteriors of comets. However, this is the main idea of a single paragraph—not the entire passage. The correct answer is (D).

Review the three steps to answering Main Idea questions listed in the Student Edition. Emphasize that students should pay close attention to the title, introductory blurb, and first and last paragraph of the passage. (See the gray box for more about why the first paragraph is important.)

LET'S TAKE A LOOK AT QUESTION 22 FROM YOUR PRACTICE TEST.

Tell students to read the entire poem and jot down a summary sentence. Then use the process of elimination to approach the answers. Choice (J) is far too broad; the poem is about *trees*, not nature as a whole. Choices (K) and (M) refer to specific *sections* of the poem, not the poem as a whole. The best answer is choice (L).

TEN DAYS TO THE ITBS®

Main Idea Questions

Main Idea questions ask you to identify the overall theme of the passage. These questions require you to evaluate the passage as a whole. To answer these questions, read the first and last paragraphs carefully, since these two paragraphs often introduce or summarize the main idea.

Let's take a look at question 22 from your practice test:

Trees: The Seeds

We are
given light wings,
parachutes, downy legs
that we may be carried aloft
by wind

and drop
where some kind mouse
will bury us in earth;
some squirrel will forget we are food,
leave us

to sprout
green shoots, to weave
rootlets, that we may eat
and drink and grow in time our own
small seeds

—*Myra Cohn Livingston*

 22 What is the main topic of this poem?

J Nature in the forest
K Animals' influence on seeds
L The life cycle of seeds
M The lightness of seeds

 Read the entire poem and jot down, in a phrase or brief sentence, what you think the message is. You might write down this summary sentence: "This poem is about how seeds grow into trees, and trees produce more seeds." From this summary sentence, you would see that choice (L) is the best choice.

Three Steps to Answering Main Idea Questions

1. **Read actively.** Use your scratch paper to write notes about each paragraph and a brief summary sentence after you finish the passage.

2. **Reread the title, the introductory text preceding the passage, the first paragraph, and the last paragraph.** The first paragraph often states the main idea, and the last paragraph often summarizes the points covered, so these are good places to look.

3. **Use the process of elimination.** Avoid answer choices that are overly specific, and answer choices that are too general. Both types serve as distractors.

EXERCISES

Assign the exercises on page 76 of the Student Edition. Ask students to underline the key sentences in each passage that helped them answer the question.

QUESTION 1

This question asks about the author's purpose. You can use this question to introduce **Author's Purpose** questions, which should be approached in a slightly different way than other Main Idea questions. Explain that there are many different *purposes* for writing: to amuse, to persuade, to explain, to tell a story, or to describe. (You may think of more.) Students should look for clues to determine the author's purpose.

The very first sentence suggests that the author is trying to convince us of a point. If students read on, they will find the thesis statement: *It is not a rock-and-roll movie, but a sharp portrait of Mexican-American life.* These two sentences suggest that the answer is (C).

QUESTION 2

This question is a Main Idea question, although it is stated slightly differently. Here, the first sentence states the main idea: Managers are paying more attention to their employees. The rest of the paragraph just elaborates on why they should pay more attention, and the final sentence sums up this information. Choice (J) is correct answer.

STRUCTURE AND AUTHOR'S STRATEGIES QUESTIONS

Structure questions ask students how a passage is developed or organized. Students need to determine if the author is illustrating a single point, listing examples, presenting an argument, comparing or contrasting events, or using some other strategy. (Examples in the Practice Test are questions 13 and 36.)

Author's Strategies questions ask students to determine why the author made certain stylistic choices—why the author included a specific phrase, or broke lines of poetry in a certain way. (Some examples in the Practice Test are questions 29, 30, and 35.)

TEN DAYS TO THE ITBS®

Exercises

Directions: Read each excerpt and answer the question that follows it.

> Most people are wrong about the film *La Bamba*. It is not a rock-and-roll movie, but a sharp portrait of Mexican-American life. Ritchie Valens came from a poor, troubled immigrant family, and when his song became a hit, he found himself instantly catapulted into stardom. Along the way, he achieved a very American dream of success and wealth. He also experienced the stresses that accompany such a transformation. The movie sensitively depicts Valens's experience, revealing his struggles and triumphs as a person.

1 What appears to be the author's purpose in this article?

  A To show the reason the song was so popular

  B To explain where Ritchie Valens got his musical talent

  C To argue that the movie was not only entertaining but also insightful

  D To explain how all immigrants have the same dreams

> Managers are becoming more responsive to the one group that can have the greatest impact on their companies' future success—the employees. Traditionally, companies have "managed down," telling employees what to do and not asking them for input. Workers, however, are usually the ones most knowledgeable about the problems that need to be fixed. When workers have been ignored, productivity has been lost. The companies that do listen have benefited greatly.

2 The paragraph mainly describes

  J the value of managers consulting employees about their jobs.

  K the pressure on managers to change.

  L the ways to fix social, economic, and political problems.

  M workers' responsibilities to their companies.

HELPFUL HINT

Situation, Solution, Resolution

The text on Eastman and many others contain the same pattern.

Situation: The author presents a problem that needs to be resolved.

Solution: The author presents ways that the problem was dealt with.

Resolution: The author shows what happens when the solution is applied.

FOR FURTHER PRACTICE

Ask students to identify other passages in the Practice Test that have this general structure.

PRACTICE PASSAGES

On pages 77–79 of the Student Edition, you will find some sample texts followed by questions. They will give students further practice in approaching Reading Comprehension texts and questions.

Encourage students to take summary notes on scratch paper.

Students' summary sentences for the Eastman passage might look something like this:

Paragraph 1: Eastman introduced new camera—cheap and easy to use.

Paragraph 2: Named it Kodak; became popular.

Paragraph 3: Still, too expensive.

Paragraph 4: Eastman improved further—made higher quality, smaller cameras.

Summary phrase: Eastman's camera: why it was so revolutionary.

QUESTION 1

Choice (C) is best. The other statements, though true, are too specific and not as significant.

QUESTION 2

Choice (J) is best. The details in the second paragraph explain that people liked the simplicity and convenience of this new camera.

Practice Passages

Directions: Read the following passage on photography and answer the questions below and on the next page.

(from They All Laughed *by Ira Flatow)*

In June 1888 Eastman introduced his revolutionary new camera. For twenty-five dollars anyone could buy one, already loaded with film. When the film was used up, the entire camera was shipped back to Rochester for processing. The film was removed, the photos developed and printed, the camera reloaded and shipped back ready to take another one hundred pictures—all for ten dollars. To help users keep track of their shots, a small memo book was packed with each camera. "You press the button, we do the rest" became the motto of the new Eastman Company.

Eastman needed a brand name for his novel camera. Finding a name for a product can be even more difficult than inventing one. Eastman knew that no matter what he called his camera, it would have to have the letter K in the name. He just happened to like that letter. The *Kodak*, easy to use, easy to spell, was introduced in 1888. It swept the country. Here was a small, lightweight camera that even a child could operate. No messy chemicals to mix. No heavy glass plates to lug around.

But the Kodak wasn't good enough. The box camera was too expensive. For fifteen dollars, a man could buy a new suit. For fifty dollars down, a five-room cottage, featuring "four closets and a full cellar" and only eighteen miles from New York City, could be purchased (total price fifteen hundred dollars).

And the paper-based film nagged at Eastman's sense of quality. So in 1889 he marketed the first transparent roll film, made from cellulose. Then came smaller and smaller cameras: the pocket Kodak in 1895 and the folding pocket Kodak in 1897 (considered the ancestor of all modern roll cameras).

1 Which of the following was most significant about Eastman's invention?

A It used glass plates at first.

B He invented the name "Kodak."

C It simplified photography for everyone.

D The camera was shipped back to Rochester for processing.

2 Why did Eastman choose the motto "You press the button, we do the rest"?

J He knew that people thought photography was too complicated.

K He wanted to explain the company's responsibilities.

L It showed the quality of the pictures.

M It explained the good value of the camera.

QUESTION 3

Choice (C) is best. The second paragraph tells us that Eastman wanted a name with the letter *K*.

QUESTION 4

Choice (L) is best. In paragraph 3, the author lists examples to prove how expensive the Kodak seemed back then.

QUESTION 5

Choice (B) is best. Paragraph 2 tells us that the original Kodak was lightweight and that camera users didn't have to worry about chemicals or glass plates. Answers (A), (C), and (D) can be eliminated.

★ EXTRA ACTIVITY

Tell students to reread the passages on Mason and Eastman (pages 32 and 77 of the Student Edition). Discuss strategies the authors used to make events of the story unfold dramatically, and brainstorm other ways to hold a reader's interest when telling a story.

Ask students to choose a 20th century invention, research how and why it was invented, and write an essay. (Tell them to use the "Situation, Solution, Resolution" pattern described on the previous page.) Present the best essays to the class, and have students discuss why they are effective.

TEN DAYS TO THE ITBS®

3 Which of the following might have Eastman chosen as the name of his camera?

- **A** Cellulose
- **B** Eastman
- **C** Koala
- **D** Rochester

4 How does the author show how expensive the Kodak was to buy in 1888?

- **J** By simply telling that it cost twenty-five dollars
- **K** By explaining how the camera was reloaded for ten dollars
- **L** By giving examples of other items and their costs back then
- **M** By showing the value of getting one hundred pictures for only ten dollars

5 Why did the paper film nag at "Eastman's sense of quality"?

- **A** Paper film got messy chemicals on the user's hands.
- **B** Paper film produced inferior pictures.
- **C** Paper film was not as stiff as glass plates.
- **D** Paper film was too heavy.

NOTES

EXTRA ACTIVITY

Have students bring their favorite multiple-paneled comic strip to class. These generally appear in the Saturday or Sunday editions of most newspapers.

Have students write a new story or new dialogue to accompany the comic strip pictures. Direct students to write a Main Idea question for their new story.

Have students swap stories and questions with their classmates. Students should then read the stories and answer each other's questions.

QUESTION 1

Choice (D) is best. The verb *eat* is being used figuratively; Louie *ate* words by reading them.

QUESTION 2

Choice (L) is best. This phrase illustrates a general point—that Louie is obsessed with words.

QUESTION 3

Choice (B) is best. *Less than right* is a tricky way of saying *wrong*.

QUESTION 4

Choice (L) is best. The last paragraph reveals something new—while all the other children speak their answers, Louie writes them. Students know from the first two paragraphs that Louie is confident, bold, and a whiz at vocabulary, so they can eliminate (J), (K), and (M). Most likely, Louie doesn't speak because he *can't*.

TEN DAYS TO THE ITBS®

Directions: Read the following passage and answer the questions below.

Louie devoured words. He swallowed them in all forms—novels, newspapers, poems, magazines, cereal boxes, comics old and new, National League baseball cards. Whatever words crossed his vision, he chewed them thoroughly, swallowed, and they became part of him. Only when he slept soundly, did Louie not chew. Even then, buckets of fried verbs and double-nounburgers filled his dreams.

Louie's teacher knew his appetite to wolf down words was so stunning that the whole town should see it. All the townspeople came to the spelling bee so that the spellers could show everyone what they could spell. There stood Louie on stage with the others. Fidgeting and twisting, the others spoke aloud their answers. Some were right, and some were less than right.

Then came Louie's turn to spell. Louie, being Louie, responded like only Louie could. He took a pen and printed his word on a pad—and won. Then he won again, and again, till he won it all. Everyone could see it. Louie had gulped down more words than anyone, and never spoke them aloud.

1 Which of the following would Louie most likely "eat"?

A A television show
B A radio program
C A movie
D A sign

2 What is the meaning of the phrase "buckets of fried verbs and double-nounburgers filled his dreams"?

J Louie wanted chicken and hamburgers.
K Louie did not have dinner.
L Louie thought about words all the time.
M Louie thought about food too much.

3 At the spelling bee, if a contestant's answer is "less than right," then that person would be

A never correct.
B incorrect this time.
C in second place.
D not allowed to answer.

4 Why doesn't Louie say the words aloud?

J He does not want to say them aloud.
K The words are difficult to pronounce correctly.
L He does not have the ability to speak.
M He is afraid to make a mistake.

Grade 6/Level 12 **PAGE 79** Ten Days to the ITBS®
